Against the Odds

Against the Odds

*Insights from
One District's
Small School Reform*

LARRY CUBAN
GARY LICHTENSTEIN
ARTHUR EVENCHIK
MARTIN TOMBARI
KRISTEN POZZOBONI

HARVARD EDUCATION PRESS
CAMBRIDGE, MASSACHUSETTS

Library of Congress Control Number: 2009942743

Paperback ISBN 978-1-934742-46-4
Library Edition ISBN 978-1-934742-47-1

Published by Harvard Education Press,
an imprint of the Harvard Education Publishing Group

Harvard Education Press
8 Story Street
Cambridge, MA 02138

Cover Design: Sarah Henderson

The typefaces used in this book are Sabon for text and ITC Stone Sans for display.

Contents

Preface

Beginning in 2004, the Mapleton Public Schools in Colorado initiated a bold, districtwide reform by converting its traditional high school into several small schools.* At that time, small school reform had gained momentum in the state and throughout the country, but to our knowledge, no other district had created small schools as the sole option for all its high school students. In early 2006, Superintendent Charlotte Ciancio approached Gary Lichtenstein, head of Quality Evaluation Designs (QED), about "documenting" the reform. The project would be funded by a grant from the Bill & Melinda Gates Foundation. The implication was that the Gates Foundation wanted to use Mapleton as an example for other districts contemplating a similarly extensive small school reform.

Initially, Lichtenstein mulled over what "documenting" might mean. It appeared that the Mapleton effort reflected the highest ideals of the small school movement. Ciancio had already spoken around the country about the district's "reinvention," which aimed to turn one of the lowest-performing districts in Colorado into one of the highest. By 2006, Mapleton had embarked on the second year of a three-year implementation plan, and most of the start-ups were going smoothly. One school struggled with personnel problems and closed, but reopened with new staff, an altered culture, and a new direction. Overall, district and

---

*Skyview High School consisted of the main high school, with approximately fourteen hundred students, and an alternative school, which enrolled approximately three hundred. Although the alternative school was housed in a separate building, its students took classes at Skyview, and the district regarded it as one of Skyview's programs. For the purposes of this book, our references to Skyview High School should be understood to include the alternative high school.

school administrators, faculty, and students were excited about the promise of small school reform. Indeed, beginning in 2006–07, the district planned to transform its elementary schools into several small schools.

And yet, as Lichtenstein visited the schools and talked with administrators, teachers, students, and staff, it became clear that the transition wasn't easy. Underlying a general mood of optimism were signs of fatigue among some teachers and outright resentment among some students. Educators in Mapleton expressed both excitement about improved relationships in their learning environments and frustration about certain administrative details and the challenges involved in creating schools that faithfully reflected the models they were intended to replicate.

The tensions underlying Mapleton's transformation contrasted with the zealous rhetoric of small school reform on the national level, but they reminded Lichtenstein of his own experiences in the field. An advocate of small schools himself, he had spent two years as director of research and evaluation at the Colorado Small Schools Initiative (CSSI), one of the Gates Foundation's intermediary organizations. CSSI was a major stakeholder in the conversion of Denver's Manual High School into three small schools, one of the nation's most spectacular small school reform failures. He came away from the experience shaken by the pain that the effort had caused to students, school personnel, and the community, in spite of the hard work and good intentions of most of those who had been involved.

Lichtenstein felt that Mapleton had proceeded skillfully with its reform—moving quickly and thoughtfully through planning and initial implementation and welcoming its external partners' expertise without conceding authority. Administrators, staff, and many students felt optimistic about the reform and pointed enthusiastically to its successes. Yet even in Mapleton, where it appeared that so much had been done right, challenges—in some cases, significant challenges—persisted. Lichtenstein had encountered some of these challenges at Manual, and knew that they had arisen in other reform efforts around the country.

Upon reflection, it seemed to Lichtenstein that there was indeed a lot to learn from looking closely at small school reform in Mapleton.

An examination of the issues that arise when a district shifts to small schools might temper the sometimes overzealous claims and expectations of small school advocates, and provide a thoughtful ground on which to build reforms that would avoid common obstacles and anticipate inevitable ones.

It was that intention which gave rise to this book. Ciancio supported the idea, even while recognizing her district's potential vulnerability. She was heartened by Larry Cuban's participation. She knew of his extensive work in school reform and his experience as a school superintendent, and she hoped that getting to know him would help her navigate some of the issues the district faced in implementing small schools. Almost immediately, the two of them forged a warm, yet candid, professional relationship. Lichtenstein then went on to recruit the rest of the research team. The methodology used to document and analyze the Mapleton initiative is described in the appendix.

We are indebted to Superintendent Charlotte Ciancio and her executive team for their courage in laying open their district to the scrutiny we have given it. To the extent that our project created more work for them, we appreciate their support and, at times, forbearance. Our interviews required the valuable time and assistance of teachers and administrators throughout the district. Students we approached were willing and even eager to share their experiences. The perspectives of board members, community members, external partners, and state officials were also invaluable. We are grateful to each of the many stakeholders who participated in this project for their candor and insights.

We are grateful to the Bill & Melinda Gates Foundation for funding, and to Sally Vincent, Molly Wolff, and Jami Loree for technical assistance. Special gratitude to Lichtenstein's good friends at the Recapture Lodge in Bluff, Utah—the Hooks, Jackie, Dawn—for their ever-generous material and emotional support.

This book is dedicated to the memory and spirit of Mr. Chris Belshe of the Manual Education Complex, and to all those school and district practitioners who muster the will and the courage to try new approaches for the sake of their students.

June 2009

Against the Odds

Introduction

So much has been written and said about urban school reform. On one side, ever-growing numbers of advocates have proposed measures to transform mediocre classrooms, rescue low-performing schools, and turn around failing districts. Those who promote these reforms are motivated by several compelling objectives: to save children from dismal futures, bolster the economy, combat social injustice, and foster democratic values. Yet the abundant exhortations for urban school reform are counterbalanced by a massive literature that documents failed efforts and paltry results. We are very much aware of that literature. In this book, we seek to sidestep the hype of reform's most ardent proponents, on the one hand, and the doom-saying of its severest critics, on the other.[1]

Against the Odds documents the launching of a fundamental school reform, the cheerful promise of change, and its zigzag implementation in a small, urban, largely minority and low-income district near Denver, Colorado. The Mapleton Public Schools struggled for nearly twenty years with declining test scores and graduation rates; by 2001, the district was one of the lowest-performing in the state. In response, a new superintendent spearheaded the conversion of Mapleton's comprehensive high school (and, eventually, of ten elementary and middle schools) into a network of small schools. The results of this transformation are simultaneously surprising, hopeful, uneven, and, in some instances, still uncertain.

In this book, we focus on the initial phase of the Mapleton reform: the creation of several small high schools.[2] The story we tell is filled with successes, but also with mishaps and persistent dilemmas. For just this reason, we think it is a story with valuable lessons for other districts contemplating small school reform.

In some respects, the circumstances in which the Mapleton reform occurred may appear singularly favorable. The school board was firmly and unanimously committed to improving the district's performance. It hired a homegrown superintendent and gave her carte blanche to implement a plan that would raise student achievement. The district had a $10 million budget surplus to fund the reform, as well as the promise of millions of dollars of support from the Bill & Melinda Gates Foundation. It is rare for the stars favoring reform to be so nicely aligned.

Yet even with this fortuitous combination of luck and leadership, the district faced both predictable and unexpected obstacles in dismantling a comprehensive high school, revising nearly all of its standard operating procedures, and importing seven national school models within three years. The superintendent and her executive team constantly faced situations in which they had to make trade-offs between competing values. They struggled to preserve the ideals of the reform, and to maintain enthusiasm among teachers, students, staff, and community members, even as they responded to disappointments and setbacks.

Mapleton is one of more than four hundred small, urban school systems in the United States.[3] Any of these districts, we believe, would have encountered similar dilemmas while trying to implement genuine, pervasive reform. Indeed, we would argue that such dilemmas are inevitable in any district, large or small, committed to the kind of transformation that Mapleton achieved.

No amount of money or hope can spare districts the challenges associated with fundamental reform. Business-inspired policy makers and foundation leaders talk about return on investment and incubating innovations, only to discover that making substantial changes in schools is more complicated than running Microsoft or Intel. Mayors take over school districts from elected school boards, only to find themselves constrained by a welter of stakeholders, laws, and policies more difficult to negotiate than they had imagined. Dynamic, tough-talking superintendents quickly institute dramatic reforms, then exit just as quickly because they lose political capital or lack the endurance to tackle day-to-day issues arising from those reforms. Private foundations set out believing that millions of dollars and elite teams of consultants can overcome the systemic problems that plague urban schools, only to discover that their interventions have yielded little or no improvement in academic outcomes.[4]

What makes school reform so tough—even in a small district of sixteen schools and roughly five thousand students? The short answer is that devising and implementing reforms in public schools, and securing the resources to fund those reforms, is a political process open to many stakeholders who have strong value differences about what ought to happen in schools and classrooms. These differences in strongly held values produce the tensions and dilemmas that accompany reforms, including those aimed at creating small schools.

Unfortunately, reformers and other stakeholders often interpret these dilemmas as evidence of resistance and failure, rather than as the inevitable concomitants of major systemic change. As a result, the energy and funding required to sustain reforms begin to wane. Yet these dilemmas cannot be prevented—instead, they must be anticipated and carefully managed. Any public school district that seeks, as Mapleton did, to reinvent its schools will confront dilemmas such as these:

- Does small school autonomy trump adherence to district standards?

- Can a district uphold a lofty vision and yet effectively manage the conflicting imperatives and logistical challenges of its daily operations?

- Does pressure by state officials for improved student achievement on standardized tests preclude thoughtful implementation of reforms and allow sufficient time to accurately assess whether the reforms are working?

These dilemmas and others lie in wait for reform-minded leaders eager to move ahead with small schools.

Putting new policies into practice in schools and classrooms—whether those policies are formulated by the president and Congress, a state legislature, a local school board, or a city mayor—is a far more complex, fragile, and tricky process than most observers expect. It is a process that mocks, rather than mimics, the chain-of-command structure so neatly articulated in district and state organizational charts. Multiple constituencies influence public schools, complicating decision making in ways that leaders in other fields, from business to the military, rarely have to confront.

This book confirms that implementing major reforms in an urban school system is intense and unrelenting work—not only for district administrators, but also for school leaders and teachers, central office staff, service personnel, and students themselves. As obstacles proliferate, too many districts lose heart and return to the status quo. In Mapleton, on the other hand, a small district developed a reform plan and has stuck to it. Its story offers lessons to other similar districts, and even to larger ones, about how to implement major reform and negotiate expected and unexpected challenges along the way. We believe that other districts can benefit from seeing how Mapleton reconfigured its policies and procedures in order to make small schools a reality. And we hope the Mapleton story will help other districts anticipate the dilemmas associated with small school reform and manage them successfully.

In telling this story, we have quoted at length from interviews with Superintendent Charlotte Ciancio, district personnel, students, board members, private foundation staff, and state officials. Actual names were used for Ciancio and foundation staff. All others are identified by pseudonyms, which appear in parentheses following each quotation. The use of pseudonyms enables us to honor pledges of confidentiality we made to those we interviewed, while allowing readers to tell when quotations dispersed through the text have come from a single source.

Chapter 1 sets the Mapleton experience in a national context, examining the growth of standards-based reform since the mid-1980s and the expansion of the small high school movement in the past decade. We describe how these two approaches to school improvement converged in Mapleton.

Chapters 2 and 3 sketch out early efforts by a string of superintendents to improve Mapleton's one comprehensive high school. When the school board appointed a reform-minded superintendent in 2001, new plans and policies were converted into concrete actions. We describe how district leaders chose small school models, hired teachers and principals, and restructured district administration.

Chapter 4 documents teachers' and students' perspectives on the new small high schools. In particular, we describe efforts to move from teacher-centered to student-centered instruction in Mapleton classrooms.

Chapter 5 asks the question: is the reform working? Here we look at test scores and other indicators, many of which discouraged district leaders in the early years of the reform and prompted them to make midcourse corrections.

Finally, chapter 6 summarizes the challenges involved in sustaining the reform as well as the lessons that other districts can draw from Mapleton's experience in creating a system of small schools.

CHAPTER ONE

Mapleton in Context

Cross-currents of School Reform

Las Vegas bookies are famous for laying odds on any outcome that can't be predicted with certainty—the results of a presidential election, next week's weather, which team will win the Rose Bowl. Here's a gamble that might have seemed worthy of a Las Vegas bet.

Imagine an urban school district, serving five thousand students, that has struggled for years to reverse declines in academic achievement. What are the odds that such a district, under a new superintendent's leadership, would successfully:

- Dismantle its large, comprehensive high school to create seven small high schools offering a variety of curriculum models, within three years?

- Replace its handful of neighborhood elementary schools with twelve schools of choice for kindergartners through eighth graders, within five years?

- Implement significant changes in classroom teaching and school culture?

- Meet the state's demands for improved academic performance?

Before bookmakers would estimate the prospects for such a reform, they would want to know something about the key players. In this case, the superintendent was neither an outsider to the district (large-scale reforms are generally undertaken by newcomers) nor someone experienced in such efforts. Rather, she was a rookie superintendent who had grown up attending local schools. The bookies would also want to assess the challenges that such a reform would face. They would ask how hard it is to create successful small high schools in an accountability-driven state; to implement districtwide urban school reform, even in a relatively small district; and to abolish neighborhood schools in favor of a system of parental choice. However, since few, if any, districts have attempted reforms on this scale, the bookies would have relatively little data to go on.

Of course, no bookies actually brokered this bet. Yet urban school reform is both high-stakes and risky for students, teachers, school boards, and superintendents. Since the 1980s, school reform has been driven—and constrained—by curricular standards, testing regimes, and accountability regulations. Across the nation, test scores now determine whether students receive a high school diploma, whether teachers and administrators receive merit pay and additional funding for their schools, and whether schools will be taken over by the state. As a result, the costs of a failed reform are higher than ever before.

It was, then, a real gamble for the school board and the superintendent of the Mapleton Public Schools in Colorado to commit themselves to significant—even radical—changes in the way children were educated. Before we look at their efforts in detail, it is important to understand the national context in which the district was operating.

STANDARDS-BASED REFORM

The national campaign to raise standards and strengthen accountability in public education originated in the mid-1970s.[1] This was a period of economic recession, increasing crime, and intractable poverty, especially in cities with substantial low-income and minority populations. It was also a time of deep concern about Japan's growing dominance of international markets, including the automobile and electronics industries. An emerging coalition of corporate and civic leaders attributed the nation's economic and social problems to underperforming, inefficient schools. A presidential commission distilled the widespread criticism of schools into *A Nation at Risk* (1983), a report that provoked a torrent of state-mandated reforms aimed at raising the academic performance of all students.

Gradually, however, business and civic leaders pressing for school reform learned how difficult it was to improve academic outcomes for urban students. Over a period of two decades, these leaders seized on one reform model after another, from corporate partnerships with individual schools in the 1980s, to whole school reform and charter schools in the early 1990s, to top-down systemic reform in the late 1990s. Educators pursued an equally diverse series of strategies to influence classroom teaching and learning. In spite of these efforts, low test scores rarely budged, especially at the secondary level.

Business and civic leaders, joined by most education policy makers, believed that the best kind of education would be a rigorous academic program equipping all students with broad knowledge of the world, strong interpersonal and intellectual skills, and attitudes suitable both for college and for jobs that required cooperative decision making, creative problem solving, and flexible skill sets. With these goals in mind, public officials borrowed heavily from business ideas and practices. They adopted strategies such as parental choice in order to promote competition between schools, and they insisted on standards as a tool for raising student achievement and holding schools accountable for their performance.

In standards-based reform, governors and legislatures mandated the goals and set curriculum standards that educators and students were required to meet. States then tested students to determine whether they had acquired the knowledge and skills specified in the standards. Teachers' and principals' judgments about individual student achievement became subordinate to test-based measures of schoolwide achievement. To ensure high performance on the tests, state officials rewarded students, teachers, and administrators for success and imposed penalties for failure. States also offered help to teachers and administrators to ensure that the standards were understood and put into practice.

Three assumptions drove this national reform movement. First, reformers assumed that *high academic standards would improve schooling*, producing skilled graduates who would successfully enter the workplace (thereby reducing inequalities in income distribution) and boost productivity (thereby fueling economic growth). Second, reformers assumed that schools and businesses were basically alike: *if choice and competition led to greater efficiencies in the larger, market-driven society, they would have the same effect when applied to schools.* Third, public officials and business leaders, deeply concerned about a workforce drawn increasingly from minority and immigrant populations in urban areas, assumed that *reforms with clear incentives (positive or negative) and rigorously enforced standards would provide equal educational (and later economic) opportunity* for youth from poor families. All students, regardless of background, could go to college and get high-paying jobs. By 2001, most national, state, and local policy makers, corporate executives, media leaders, educators, and parents took these three assumptions for granted. And all three assumptions were embodied in the federal No Child Left Behind (NCLB) Act, which was passed with support from both political parties and signed by President George W. Bush in 2002.

For the most part, state and local policy makers swiftly adopted the NCLB school-reform agenda. Who could argue against a program that promised greater accountability for schools receiving public funds, provided additional dollars for reading programs and other interventions targeting low-performing students, and promoted safe, drug-free schools? Those who might have been reluctant to jump on the bandwagon faced strong political pressure. Moreover, the penalty for noncompliance with the law's mandates was loss of federal funding.

Still, concerns among state officials about burdensome regulations—and especially about increases in state expenditures to meet NCLB requirements—did arise within the first three years after the law was enacted. Some states threatened to forgo federal aid rather than comply with the law; several objected to exclusive reliance on test scores to determine academic success. During debates over the reauthorization of NCLB in 2007, federal officials showed some willingness to bend and amend certain regulations. Nonetheless, the powerful rhetoric of NCLB made it difficult for opponents of the law to overturn its core provisions. Voters generally believed in the cash value of education and its larger benefits to society. They supported high academic standards, more testing, and expanded school choice to ensure that children were prepared for college and the workplace. NCLB codified popular thinking about the value of standards-based reforms and market-driven education.[2]

NCLB placed very real demands on schools and school districts to improve student achievement. As a result, the law revitalized interest in education reform. Policy makers and educators who believed that the system of public education was broken sought new approaches. One of these approaches had been around for many years and soon attracted much attention from reformers.

SMALL HIGH SCHOOL REFORM

Reforms seldom queue up and wait their turn to enter public schools. So it was that the standards movement, with its emphasis on accountability through standardized testing, overlapped with an ongoing effort by progressive-minded reformers to break up the large urban high schools where so many poor and minority students were failing academically.

Beginning in the 1980s, these reformers argued that massive comprehensive high schools—an innovation dating back to the 1920s—were ineffective because they were impersonal. Students disappeared into large schools; they became anonymous. In small schools, on the other hand, students would be "known" and therefore more likely to succeed. The reformers also argued that small schools would be better able to develop organizational structures, curricula, and instructional approaches that met their students' individual needs.[3] For this to happen, however, small schools would have to be granted significant autonomy.

The call for school-site autonomy within a district initially ran counter to the standards movement, which, as the name implies, favored uniformity in curriculum and (by implication) instruction. Nonetheless, private and public funders latched onto small high schools as a powerful means of engaging poor and minority students and thereby enabling them to reach state standards. As a result, the two reforms converged. Although they differ in their views of autonomy, their definitions of essential knowledge, their strategies for motivating students, and their vision of what ultimately counts as student success, both standards-based and progressive small-school approaches seek to improve student achievement. It was the kind of strange, unplanned connection that sometimes occurs within the amorphous, shifting marketplace of ideas in a democratic society.[4]

A Brief History of Small High Schools

Small high schools are neither new nor uniform. As far back as the 1920s, districts were creating small high schools (often called "continuation schools") for students who found larger, more traditional schools difficult to negotiate. In the late 1960s and early 1970s, however, an array of small, alternative high schools appealing to academically diverse students arose. *Magnet schools* sought to lessen de facto segregation in public education. *Free schools* offered flexible curricula that allowed students to work in small groups and on individual projects and to develop close relationships with teachers. In other cases, groups of parents and teachers created *progressive schools* committed to equity and social justice, where poor and minority students could learn in innovative ways. All of these small, alternative schools operated as schools of choice.[5]

The research literature analyzing these schools indicated that size mattered. Small high schools cultivated personal relationships between adults and youth, increased students' intellectual engagement, reduced dropout rates, and created learning communities. Stories accumulated of formerly alienated students who had enrolled in small, alternative high schools and been transformed into high-achieving, college-bound graduates.[6] Indeed, nearly all of the students in successful small schools graduated and entered four-year colleges and universities.[7]

Relatively few of these schools, however, were still operating by the end of the 1970s. Those that survived were able to adapt to the ever-changing demands of parents and district administrators, while remaining the kind of schools that students and teachers embraced.

Then, in the 1980s and early 1990s, a new generation of small schools emerged. Several were part of a national network, the Coalition of Essential Schools (CES), founded by Theodore Sizer. In New York City, two large high schools were replaced by eleven small schools through a partnership between the board of education and the nonprofit Center for Collaborative Education. Like their earlier counterparts, these small high schools were committed to the principle of choice, to progressive curriculum and instruction, and to education for democracy and social justice. And they each had sufficient autonomy to decide for themselves how best to pursue their goals.[8]

As federal, state, and local policy makers embraced standards-based testing and accountability in the mid-1990s, small high schools further differentiated. This trend accelerated after the Bill & Melinda Gates Foundation, the wealthiest foundation in the world, dedicated itself to tackling what it identified as two of the world's biggest problems: AIDS in Africa and high schools in America. The Gates Foundation determined that small schools were the key to improving secondary education in the United States. Since 1999, the foundation has made education grants totaling more than $1.4 billion, most of which has gone toward creating small high schools (defined as no larger than four hundred students). A variety of small high schools appeared, some as "small learning communities" within large high schools, others as freestanding ones in separate facilities.

At a governors' summit in 2005, Bill Gates reasserted the rationale for this ambitious reform:

America's high schools are obsolete.

By obsolete, I don't just mean that they're broken, flawed or underfunded, though a case could be made for every one of those points.

By obsolete, I mean our high schools—even when they're working as designed—cannot teach all our students what they need to know today.[9]

With Gates funding, more than two thousand comprehensive high schools have been converted to small schools. Such an infusion of private money into public education is unprecedented in U.S. history. Meanwhile, hundreds of charter schools, urban academies, and for-profit small schools have opened across the country, often with philanthropic support. As a result, a stunning spectrum of all kinds of high schools now exists.

The Research on Small Schools

As private foundation dollars accelerated the movement to create small urban public high schools, accountability policies were entering a period of ascendancy. After nearly two decades of standards-based reform at the state level, NCLB pressed local districts to raise student performance on state tests. Each state could choose the test it would use to measure progress, but the law mandated that, whatever the test, schools demonstrate progress toward the goal of having all students demonstrate proficiency by 2014. Schools that do not make Adequate Yearly Progress (AYP) toward that goal are labeled as failing and are subject to sanctions if they continue to fall below the federal standard.

Applying standards-based policies and testing requirements to small high schools was bound to create dilemmas for reformers. For example, how far should small high schools committed to project-based learning and writing-based assessments go in order to prepare students for state tests consisting of multiple-choice questions? With district officials calling for greater uniformity in curriculum and instruction in order to meet NCLB and state accountability requirements, how much curricular and operational autonomy should small high school principals and faculties enjoy? These questions reveal the tensions that occur when two reforms converge.[10] But such tensions were often ignored, at least initially, by reformers touting the successes of small high schools and by district officials welcoming an abundant flow of monies into their coffers.

Meanwhile, the evidence supporting the establishment of small urban high schools received little close scrutiny during the reform's early years. Champions of small schools rested their case, to a significant extent, on the well-documented flaws of the large urban schools they wished to replace. Small schools were celebrated as alternatives to schools where students were lost in the crowd; where curriculum and instruction were ill-suited to individual interests and aspirations; where students feared for their safety; and where uninspiring, inexperienced teachers were strangers to their students' communities and cultures. These are the ills that small schools set out to address, and numerous case studies, both of alternative schools from the 1970s and of newer small schools, indicated their success in doing so.

In the research literature, one finds repeated claims that, compared to comprehensive high schools, small high schools have attained the following outcomes:

- Personalized instruction

- Increased student attendance and graduation rates

- Increased teacher satisfaction

- Reduced incidence of violence or disruptive behavior

- Improved school climate

- Greater cost-effectiveness

- Improved student achievement[11]

Three cautions about these claims are in order, however.

First, there is no one kind of small high school. Small schools vary widely in their organizational structures, curricula, and instructional styles.

Second, the research cited in favor of small schools often relies on case studies. With so much variation among these schools, care must be taken to determine how representative the school chosen for a case study may be. Further, there has been little research comparing students who attend small high schools with students similar in background and achievement who attend comprehensive high schools.

Third, while numerous studies have shown strong correlations between smaller high school size (defined as enrollment well below one thousand) and most of the outcomes listed above, the research to date has *not* produced conclusive evidence for the last, critical outcome—

increased student achievement. To the extent that evidence of higher achievement has been offered, researchers have not demonstrated that the effects are attributable to small schools per se, rather than, say, to the income level of the students who attend them.[12]

Claims that small high schools will improve test scores and reduce the achievement gap between minority and white students are contested within the research community. No consensus on this point now exists among scholars. After reviewing the literature on school size, Linda Darling-Hammond et al. concluded, "The evidence is more mixed with respect to achievement effects of school size [than for other outcomes], raising the questions, 'Smaller (or larger) than what?' and 'for whom?'"[13]

While Darling-Hammond and her colleagues chose their words carefully, other researchers have enthusiastically attributed academic gains to small schools without specifying the design and methodology of their studies, controlling for key variables, or stating the size of the alleged effects on academic achievement. Meanwhile, skeptics point to studies denying that test scores or other measures of academic achievement increase among students attending small schools.[14]

Perhaps it is still too soon to judge the academic effects of small high schools. Bill Gates, however, has already made up his mind. In his "First Annual Letter" (2009), he wrote, "Many of the small high schools we invested in did not improve students' achievement in any significant way."[15] The Gates Foundation now draws a contrast between small high schools' success in achieving desirable non-academic outcomes and their limited academic impact: "Results from evaluations of foundation-funded schools show that new, small schools can improve school climate, grade progression, and student attendance. Improved graduation rates do not always mean greater student achievement or college readiness."[16]

Small school reform is not as widespread as it was ten years ago, largely because the Gates Foundation is no longer funding such initiatives. Moreover, some districts that implemented small school conversions have reversed course and gone back to operating large, comprehensive high schools. Nonetheless, there are plenty of district and school leaders who still believe in the promise of small schools. New York City Chancellor Joel Klein, for example, insists that his small schools have fostered improvements in academic performance as well as in attendance, retention, and school climate. For reasons we will explore further in chapter 5, we believe that it is probably too soon to make definitive judgments about the potential of small schools to improve the academic performance and life chances of urban youth.[17]

Both academic and nonacademic outcomes continue to be cited as reasons to replace large high schools with small ones, particularly in urban centers. Certainly these were among the reasons cited by Mapleton officials when they made their gamble on small schools. The district was committed to engaging students, changing school culture, and raising student achievement. In this era of test-based accountability, the Colorado Department of Education was especially insistent on that last outcome.

The unfolding national picture of two distinct but overlapping reforms provides the context for Mapleton's reinvention of its secondary schools. In Mapleton, energetic, committed leaders combined the standards movement's emphasis on high expectations and accountability with the small school movement's emphasis on personalization, student-centered instruction, and participatory democracy. The chapters that follow trace the course of this ambitious reform.

CHAPTER TWO

The Origins of the Reform

The Mapleton Public Schools (MPS) had once been known for providing children with a high-quality education. Many of the district's teachers and administrators had grown up in Mapleton and were at home in the community. They maintained strong relationships with parents and gave children individual attention. As one classified employee, a Mapleton native, explained:

> When I started with the school district [in 1976, it was] . . . more like a family-oriented place. We didn't have a lot of people moving in and out of the neighborhoods. We knew the teachers . . . They're still friends of mine. [They would say to me], "You know, your daughter is not doing real well in this class," and "Is there anything that we can do to help her out?" . . . We had that real close communication.

Along with its small-town atmosphere, the district was known for its willingness to support creative approaches in the classroom. As a result, it attracted teachers and administrators who were seeking opportunities for innovation.

Despite these strengths, Mapleton's standardized achievement test scores flattened and then declined throughout the 1980s and 1990s. On the nationally administered Comprehensive Tests of Basic Skills (CTBS),

MPS students on average scored consistently between the 40th and 50th percentiles. These scores were surprisingly resistant to improvement and often showed small declines from year to year. A former Mapleton high school principal described the frustration generated by this underachievement:

> Whatever standardized tests we used to give, [the overall score] would go up two, down two; up three, down four . . . never making any real significant gains, no matter what little thing you tried that was different. "Oh, let's do two sections of math." Every kid takes two sections of math every semester. Math scores: low and flat. "Let's have them take a reading class and a language arts class." Reading scores: low and flat . . . We just didn't see anything that we were doing that was making a difference. (Moore)

Apart from low test scores, there were other signs that Mapleton students were faltering. During the 1980s and early 1990s, fewer than 50 percent of the district's ninth-graders ultimately graduated from Skyview High School—and this wasn't because students were moving out of the district. The dropout problem was accompanied by declining attendance and rising truancy. Students' low expectations for themselves were also a source of concern. According to one MPS educator, it was not unusual to hear students say, "I can't wait until I graduate from high school, and then I've pretty much met it—met my goal."

These low expectations were shared by some of Mapleton's teachers, counselors, and administrators. When asked to explain why test scores were flat or why students were disengaged, staff at the high school often responded that the schools were doing as well as could be expected. As one administrator reported, many MPS educators said openly that the students were performing adequately, "considering their backgrounds." One evaluator, assessing reform efforts of the 1980s and 1990s, put it bluntly: "Mapleton has a long history of providing options for kids that aren't academically challenging."[1]

Charlotte Ciancio remembers confronting low staff expectations during her first tour of the district as superintendent:

The first year, the 2001–2002 year, we went to every school and talked to staff, and we'd say, "What's been happening? What have you learned? Tell me how you got to where you are." The high school staff . . . did say to me, "Given who our kids are, we're doing damn good." I was very offended. I said to them at that very first staff meeting, "You know, every time you say that, you're talking about me. You're acting incredibly rude. I don't know where you guys grew up, but I grew up here. These kids are no different than me. They have the same chance in life that I have." I guess I left [with] that feeling that these aren't people who hold the values [that I do].

From the start, Ciancio identified with the new generation of Mapleton students: "These kids are no different than me." Yet there had been significant changes in the community since she had graduated from the local schools. Over the previous two decades, Mapleton had changed from a farming community of predominantly blue-collar Anglo families to an urban community that was nearly two-thirds Latino. Before this demographic shift occurred, there were few signs of urbanization or industrialization in Mapleton. It was a city of small truck farms, gravel roads, and vegetable stands:

There was very little white collar, very little executives. It was hardworking people, salt of the earth. Believed in education—saw it as a chance for kids to move forward. My grandfather had a truck farm over on 80th and York that had been the poor farm, and they bought it when they came from the old country. And [now] that's right in the middle of Mapleton." (Gregory, former superintendent of a neighboring school district)

As the city's residents prospered, many of them moved to Denver and its suburbs. Farmland passed into the hands of developers, who built inexpensive apartment complexes. Soon, recent immigrants to the United States—mostly Latinos, but some Asians as well—moved in. As a result, MPS became a predominantly Latino school district. A population that had been stable for decades became more transient, and poverty became more prevalent. By the 1980s, a mix of Latino migrant workers and white-collar whites seeking larger, less expensive homes than could be bought in Denver had settled in the area. This influx dramatically altered the demographic mix of children in local school districts, including MPS.

Over the next two decades, the district's enrollment fell from over six thousand to just over five thousand students. Nearly two-thirds of these students were Latino (including many English language learners), and over half were eligible for free or reduced-price lunch. Superintendents and school boards wrestled with the effects of changes in the school population as well as with increased state and federal demands for improved academic achievement. By 2000, scores on the state test (Colorado State Assessment Program, or CSAP) and a national college admission exam (ACT) were plummeting, and so were high school graduation rates. As these results garnered publicity, the school board and its superintendents cast about for explanations. Critics identified the usual suspects: insufficient district planning, superintendents coming and going, and underprepared students.

Eventually, the demographic shift in Mapleton and the district's slow pace in adapting to it became the standard explanation for the slide in school performance. A former principal's statement is typical:

> I was in one of the schools [where] the population changed, when all of a sudden we went from mainly English speakers to Spanish speakers . . . We did know we needed to change, [but] we weren't quite sure how to change . . . When you get a second-language student, they're certainly as smart as any other student. But they need a different kind of education to progress. (Jones)

Not only were the students changing, but so were the teachers. Some had retired, and many of those who remained were disillusioned:

> At parties I'd hear them talking about the old days as compared to now. Teachers felt there had been a significant change in the population they were serving. Certainly with poverty. But also . . . a willingness to want to learn, a willingness to connect in education—they didn't see that . . . And what they had done, I think, [was] say, "I'm

going to teach the kids who really are motivated, and I'm going to teach the kids who want to be here." (Gregory)

By the late 1990s, there was almost universal agreement among teachers, administrators, and community leaders that the status quo was untenable. The catalyst for reform came from the high school students' poor performance on the state-mandated CSAP, first administered in 1997. The CSAP results in reading, writing, and math were disheartening, to say the least. Mapleton students were scoring in the 40th percentile in reading and the 10th percentile in math—even lower than they had scored on the nationally normed Comprehensive Tests of Basic Skills (CTBS).

Although the CTBS had consistently shown that MPS students were underachieving in comparison with national norms, CSAP demonstrated that they were underachieving in comparison with Colorado norms as well. A former school board member commented: "I would have thought we could have performed at least at average. And we were several points below average in a lot of areas . . . So we as a board were looking into the results and saying, 'What else can we do? Because what we're doing isn't working.'" (Stevenson)

A local business leader expressed his concerns even more strongly:

[T]he test scores were frightening. They were bad. And they [MPS] hadn't had the leadership to take a look and say, "Yikes! . . . We just can't do this!" . . . When I was at school in Mapleton, we felt like it was a good school, like we were getting a good education—something that we could build on and move forward in our lives with. And I think the feeling around the community, at least in the recent past, is that [this] wasn't occurring. It wasn't a school district [where] kids were getting educated, for whatever reason. (Franco)

EARLY ATTEMPTS AT HIGH SCHOOL REFORM

In fact, during the two decades before Charlotte Ciancio became superintendent, the district had made several attempts at reform. In the

1980s, for example, dissatisfaction with students' test performance sparked an interest in the work of Ted Sizer and the Coalition of Essential Schools (CES).[2] MPS joined a network of Colorado schools seeking to implement CES principles. The district then embarked on a strategic planning process with large numbers of educators and significant community involvement. Committees produced hopeful documents that were highlighted at school board meetings for a few months and then shelved. Unfortunately, this became the pattern in Mapleton. New superintendents—there were four between 1979 and 2001—developed strategic plans and introduced programs, many of which lasted a few years and then disappeared when the school board hired another superintendent. Academic achievement and graduation rates continued to sag.

A more limited reform effort met a similar fate. In the early 1980s, a group of teachers and the principal at Skyview, the district's only comprehensive high school, obtained a grant to plan a small "school within a school," based on CES principles. Nothing happened. By the end of the decade, the principal had obtained a second grant to study reform proposals, teachers and administrators were attending national conferences, and groups of teachers had developed a plan to create as many as four small high schools in Mapleton. But in 1996 a new superintendent decided that small school reform was too radical. Instead, the district would retain Mapleton's comprehensive high school and focus on standards-based instruction.

Nevertheless, the notion that a more personalized approach was needed to raise student achievement never disappeared from MPS, and the late 1990s saw continuing efforts to implement small school principles at Skyview. One principal created instructional teams to develop standards and assessments and to improve curricular integration. Skyview also adopted block scheduling in order to increase instructional time and give teachers more opportunities for collaborative planning. Other initiatives, specifically targeting low-achieving students, followed the first reports of low CSAP scores in 1997. AVID, a highly regarded program to promote college readiness, was integrated into the Skyview curriculum.[3] Administrators met regularly with struggling students during advisory periods, tracked their classroom performance, and got parents involved in planning and supporting their children's education.

The school board hired Ciancio's predecessor with the explicit purpose of boosting test scores. Dynamic and innovative, this superintendent was a strong proponent of using student performance data to guide instruction. She instituted fine-grained measures of achievement and strongly advocated frequent, ongoing assessment of student learning. As one current Mapleton educator explained:

> She had a great, strong personality, and she could create energy and passion and pull people along with her . . . She had her own ideas about what ought to happen, and so she would make sure those things happened. So we improved the assessment process, broadened the assessment process. She really went after instructional procedures . . . Unfortunately, it [the reform] was random and pretty much defined by the things that mattered to her . . . I don't mean to be critical of that, because those things were important and they moved us forward. But they weren't driven by an overall plan. (Masterson)

Despite the changes, students did not make the steady gains that Mapleton's school board and executive leaders expected. There were pockets of improvement, but not the broad gains in test scores necessary to meet state requirements for student performance.

Although the period prior to Ciancio's superintendency was marked by vigorous efforts to reform the Mapleton schools, these efforts had been directed toward improving the existing instructional program, not radically reinventing the system:

> There were a lot of things that the district was trying to do . . . that should have worked. We changed even the reading program. We went to Success for All at a couple of different schools to try to address declining reading scores—with no results. We brought in consultants . . . What I remember from my place at the table was constant innovation, constant effort to do something . . . within the traditional educational model, and nothing making much difference . . . We couldn't figure out why things weren't working. We were doing all the

things that research said ought to be improving achievement. And we had really tweaked and really tightened and really reformed . . . So we were starting [the small school reform] with that—starting with the recognition that scores weren't going anywhere in the face of all those improvements in the traditional way of doing things, and basically saying, "OK, if that's not working with our population, then we've got to do something different." (Masterson)

Reflections about the reforms of the 1980s and 1990s coalesced around one central theme—MPS could continue to tinker with programs, but minor changes would not address declining achievement.

[O]ur belief was, at that point, it wasn't a matter of any more tightening. It had to be something else . . . Kids were not committed to their own education. The only people committed to the education were the educators, and we weren't producing the results . . . And then there was this sense of, "Maybe it's the people aspect . . . maybe it's the connection aspect that's keeping us from going where we need to go." (Masterson)

By 2001, Mapleton's leaders were ready to inaugurate an era of comprehensive reform. And with the hiring of Charlotte Ciancio as superintendent, that new era began.

DEVELOPING A VISION

Ciancio is a Mapleton native who comes from a family of ten children. She attended an MPS elementary and middle school and then a Catholic high school. After completing college and receiving a teaching credential, she taught in Mapleton elementary schools in the early 1980s, including the one she had attended as a child. Although she had been trained in progressive teaching methods—creating activity centers, making content and skills relevant to children, serving the needs of the "whole child"—Ciancio's veteran colleagues in Mapleton tried to steer her towards more traditional classroom approaches.

Eventually, Ciancio earned a master's degree in bilingual special education. She left the district for a time to teach students with disabilities in a Missouri school, but then returned to Mapleton to be a bilingual teacher. Then she secured an administrative credential. She served briefly as an assistant principal in a Mapleton elementary school, and then as an elementary school principal in an adjacent district. Soon after, she returned to MPS as executive director of learning services. During these years as a teacher and administrator, she married and had four children, all of whom attended Mapleton schools. When the district superintendent resigned in May 2001, Ciancio applied for the post, and the school board appointed her in July of that same year.

This brief sketch of Ciancio's career does not capture the intensity, vigor, and steadfast commitment of this woman in her first superintendency. With no experience as a district leader, she took office determined to make Mapleton a place where children could "achieve their dreams." Ciancio wanted to recapture the familylike feeling that she recalled from the days when she and other future MPS teachers and administrators attended district schools. Just as important, she wanted to promote high expectations for students and the constructivist classroom practices—project based, inquiry driven, harnessed to a real-world curriculum—that she had found so successful in her work as a special educator. Ciancio explained: "Most of us on the team were elementary educators . . . I guess we were trying to apply what we believed about learning theories to the context of the classroom for high school-aged kids."

To achieve its goals, the district needed a strategic plan. Ciancio's first task was to initiate a planning process that would involve all of the district's stakeholders and yield a compelling blueprint for reform.

The typical course of such efforts is all too familiar. Strategic planning sessions usually take place away from school grounds and the imperatives of day-to-day operations, sometimes in the rarefied air of pleasant conference facilities. The participants engage in energetic discussions of educational goals and principles. In the best of circumstances, they use data to clarify the challenges and opportunities facing the school district. They wrangle over words and phrases—sometimes for hours, sometimes for days and weeks. In the end, they formulate a document that is adopted by the school board and that serves, for a time, as a justification for change.

In most districts, however, change remains elusive. A strategic plan may be printed up and posted in the district office and the schools, but soon it is obscured by the weekly memo or the monthly lunch menu. Few proposed reforms are actually implemented—and those that *are* implemented may be severely weakened by the compromises necessary to win acceptance from all the affected parties. In the end, the beacon of reform becomes a dim bulb, and the new system is barely distinguishable from the one that the strategic plan promised to overthrow.[4]

Ciancio and her executive team were aware of these challenges when they selected Bill Cook to lead a three-day planning session in Estes Park, Colorado, in April 2002. Among school leaders throughout Colorado, Cook was a highly regarded planner, and he had worked with Mapleton administrators in the past.

More than 150 people attended the Estes Park session, including most of the principal stakeholders in Mapleton: parents, teachers, administrators, classified staff, community leaders, and school board members. One board member described the process in these terms: "I didn't know what to expect when we went to it, but that was probably the hardest three days I ever worked in any seminar . . . We were basically running from seven in the morning until eleven at night. And Dr. Cook drove that." (Stevenson)

The participants saw that this planning effort was different from anything they had done before. Mapleton educators had "talked seriously about reform over the years," a former principal recalled. "We would go, we'd do strategic planning. I don't think we implemented it." But CSAP had raised the stakes, and participants were encouraged by their new superintendent's energy and resolve.

These three days of work produced a strategic plan with a mission statement and a set of goals for the reform. The mission statement required the district and everyone working there to re-create the schools and themselves:

MAPLETON PUBLIC SCHOOLS MISSION STATEMENT

The mission of Mapleton Public Schools, a diverse and innovative learning community deeply rooted in its history and passionately committed to the uniqueness and potential of all students, is to guarantee that each student achieves his or her dreams and contributes enthusiastically to his or her community and world, through an educational system characterized by: an unyielding commitment to academic excellence; an enticing menu of learning opportunities that allows students to pursue their interests and gifts; a commitment that no obstacle shall impede a student's success; an environment of integrity, encouragement, and caring; and a comprehensive community working collectively to ensure the success of each child.

—April 2002

In June 2002, the school board adopted the mission statement even though the strategic plan was still emerging. Like many such documents, it was printed and distributed extensively. But unlike many such documents, the MPS mission statement became a battle cry for reform and remains to this day a living document for the school board, district administrators, principals, and teachers.

It would be another nine months before administrators, teachers, and other stakeholders fully outlined the strategic plan for bringing about the goals stated in the mission. Of all the ideas expressed in the mission statement, one in particular would be ceaselessly invoked in subsequent years: MPS would offer "an enticing menu of learning opportunities that allows students to pursue their interests and gifts." This statement eventually became the justification for the small school innovations that transformed the district.

As Ciancio recalls, however, small school reform was not the first strategy contemplated for achieving the mission:

We actually started with the ideas around career academies . . . We thought about an engineering design [school], one that was a pre-med kind of science school . . . So when we first started talking career academies, that's when our research started. Who else is doing a career academy? Can we find an engineering career academy?

. . . And then I had lunch with Gary Resnick [a former colleague at Mapleton who later became a school director], and that kind of blew it up. And he was sitting there listening and telling me how impressive that was, and that he was really excited to see we were doing something different. And then he said, "Let me tell you about something that we're doing," and he was opening the Big Picture High School in Denver. And so I wanted to know more about that. He said, "Unlike the career academies that you're talking about, Charlotte, that narrow students' view of the world, our intention is to widen it. Our intention is to expand what they know today." I thought, "Dammit!" I had this sick feeling in my stomach.

I went back to [the executive team] and said, "You guys, I think we're narrowing choice!" And we couldn't find anything that supported the career academy concept. We'd all been researching it, and nobody could find anything that supported that idea at the time. But we were starting to uncover several small schools, and we were familiar with the Coalition of Essential Schools because we had that background.

And then Resnick said, "Would you like to meet these people from Big Picture?" And so we met Elliot Washor and then the Colorado Children's Campaign, and then all that started.

Of course, there are many ways that Mapleton could have provided "an enticing menu of learning opportunities" *within* a comprehensive high school. It could have increased the number and variety of electives, added programs that focused on technology or the arts, or created small learning communities within the existing building. But district leaders concluded that such measures would not allow Mapleton to achieve the vision articulated in the mission statement:

The vision says something like, we will guarantee that each student reaches his or her full potential and meets their dreams . . . I think that was the seed for the small school idea—that it's hard to meet your dreams when there's twelve hundred kids in this high school. (Meekin)

[T]he idea of a menu of options—I will never forget that term . . . [I]t wasn't choice just about, in high school, what class you took; it might be choice about how you learned. That was huge for me. (Jones)

Charlotte had always kind of said, "We've got to make sure it's real choice." Real choice means different grade levels, different programs and pedagogical sorts of things in the school, and different characteristics amongst the schools . . . We didn't want to be a bunch of small schools housed in a high school . . . having them do business as normal. (Masterson)

Other factors, too, pushed the district toward small school reform. Many Mapleton educators had been waiting for an opportunity to implement the principles advocated by Ted Sizer and the Coalition of Essential Schools. After years of trying to fine-tune the existing secondary school programs, after years of small gains and small setbacks in test scores, the time seemed right for a radical restructuring of high school education in Mapleton.

Although the small school reform was not driven by the promise of external funding, it was considered at a time when such an initiative could attract substantial financial support. As noted earlier, the Bill & Melinda Gates Foundation had committed millions of dollars to high school reform, working through local intermediaries that distributed funds and provided logistical support to schools and districts. For the MPS reform, the intermediary would be the Colorado Small Schools Initiative (CSSI), then directed by Van Schoales. CSSI did not support small learning communities, which it perceived as a compromised reform. Schoales was interested in funding distinct, autonomous small high schools:

[A]t the time in Colorado, the innovative thing was, "Well, let's break up our existing high school into smaller learning communities with themes, or small schools." I, from the get-go, was really skeptical of that working, even though that was a big part of what our grant [from the Gates Foundation] was designed to do, because of a feeling that existing high school cultures are so massive that they subsume whatever new structures or practices that you try and build.

Seeing the potential of the MPS vision and of a superintendent committed to districtwide, small school reform, CSSI approached Ciancio and offered its support. Completing an application for a planning grant seemed almost a formality—funding for exploring small school options was assured early on. Yet the process of completing the CSSI grant also determined the path of the strategic plan. Small schools would become the means by which the mission, with its "enticing menu of learning opportunities," would be accomplished. In March 2003, the Board of Education approved the strategic plan. Now Mapleton was committed to small schools. But which ones?

Shopping for Small School Models

The initial planning grant, in the amount of $35,000, enabled teams of Mapleton parents, teachers, the union president, administrators, and school board members to visit small high schools around the country. Each team had roughly ten members and made eight trips over a four-month period, from summer to early fall 2003. The teams visited Boston, New York, Chicago, San Diego, Sacramento, Napa, San Francisco, Portland (Maine), and Providence (Rhode Island). In neighborhoods with even more challenging demographics than Mapleton's, the MPS teams found public, private, and charter schools with successful track records—schools that students and parents had chosen for themselves. One principal recalled a Mapleton parent's response to the Met, the original Big Picture School in Providence:

> I remember her saying, "You guys, we have to do this. I want the things that these kids are getting for our kids." And when [school board members] see those things happening, they all say it. They don't say it all exactly the same way, but every single one of the board members says, "I'm excited. I want this for our kids. I can see that works. It's not an experiment. We need to do this." (Frank)

Other participants tell the same story. A former board member described his reaction to the Met:

What really impressed me was just sitting down talking to a couple of students and basically hearing their story . . . They're talking about going to Harvard and going to Princeton and all these Ivy League schools that you just dream of . . . and they have the academic credentials to go . . . Now, did they get in? I don't know. But at least to hear kids at that level talking intelligently in those terms was very uplifting for me. (Stevenson)

The same board member recalled her experience at Codman Academy, an Expeditionary Learning middle school outside of Boston:

[T]hey had their expectations: "Here's what we're going to learn today on the board. Here's what we're going to discuss." So it was structured. I'm looking at that [and saying], "Damn, they're discussing some very interesting topics, and intelligently." And the kids were energized to learn . . . I left there with goose bumps going up and down my back. (Stevenson)

This is not to say that the visitors lacked a critical perspective. Over time, they became increasingly sophisticated in assessing whether a given school would work in the Mapleton context. One administrator said:

After your tenth visit to a school, you get pretty savvy . . . "Okay, so what do you do with kids who have an Individual Education Plan?" And they say, "Oh, we don't have any of those kids here." And then you go, "Oh, okay." Or, "Tell us the different languages that you have at your school—not that you necessarily teach, but that your families use regularly." "Oh, we don't have any of those." You know, that kind of thing. So, we have to think about the context of our community, and we got better at talking with students and teachers rather than just being led through a school. (Moore)

After several site trips, some schools emerged as stellar models in the minds of the visiting MPS teams. Many of these models had been developed by educators committed to "whole school reform." They were consistent with the mission and goals of the Estes Park meeting, the strategic plan, and the superintendent's instructional philosophy. Team members believed that the small schools they observed were successful alternatives to Mapleton's status quo, and this led to a consensus on how to proceed:

> Our last gathering was at the office of the Boston small schools reform. We were there to try to get their take on what small schools meant and how we might be able to become a system that has small schools that are chosen. And we had a great discussion with them. It was at the end of that meeting that Charlotte simply said, after a few other words, "How many of you are in favor of what it is that we're talking about doing?" And unanimously, thumbs went up around the room . . . That amazed everybody, because we thought, "Jeez, we really are getting to the same page here." (Morrison)

After considering the logistics of the reform—space, staffing, resources, enrollment—the planning teams initially recommended that Mapleton open four small high schools: two in fall 2004, and two more in fall 2005. None would have more than one hundred students in any grade level, and all would be based on programs the teams had visited.

The school board had expressly charged Ciancio with the task of identifying school models that had already proven to be successful. It did not want district staff to start from scratch when educators elsewhere had already come up with effective programs. One staff member involved in the planning said: "Our superintendent and school board made a decision that we weren't going to invent things that were good for our kids. We were going to replicate things that were already working."

A board member made a similar point: "I didn't want to use our district or kids as guinea pigs, as an experiment . . . What I was looking for was proven educational concepts that are repeatable and go on year after year, automatic. It doesn't require a driver sitting there driving it year after year after year to make it work. It has to be something that's self-sustaining and shows results."

In selecting partners for the Mapleton reform, the planning teams asked whether each program could (1) contribute to the "enticing menu" called for in the mission statement; (2) emphasize academic *rigor*, generate curricula *relevant* to the students' lives, and promote positive *relationships* between students and between students and teachers; (3) provide adequate coaching for curriculum and staff development; (4) demonstrate success in raising graduation rates and college acceptance; and (5) accept the district's participation in and ultimate authority over deciding how a school would be administered.

On the ground, however, what observers from Mapleton were most compelled by were hopeful stories from students who were like Mapleton students and who had hopes for their future. As Ciancio expressed it:

> After seeing Big Picture [in Providence] and then Codman Academy [in Boston], we all felt we had this moral obligation to offer something different than we had been offering. I think that came from the interviews with students. We heard things from kids that had more significant challenges than the kids we work with, talking to us about success and futures and their hopes and their dreams and all the things we valued here.

Ciancio remembers meeting four Codman students who walked a mile and a half to take a gym class in a tennis club—the only facility where they could earn their physical education credits. "They were so amazing. Two of them came in from Providence—took a bus or subway or whatever to get there to Boston, because they believed in what these teachers could offer them and they had such hope for a brighter future. It just inspired everyone in the room."

CSSI director Van Schoales, who helped arrange the planning teams' visits, noted that programs such as Big Picture and Expeditionary Learning were "shoppers," too: "[E]ach of the models is looking for places where they're likely to have support for implementation of their design . . . to replicate it with some fidelity to the design. And it's hard to find districts like that. In every case, I was selling them on Mapleton as well."

Model developers found MPS an attractive replication site. Since most had launched their programs as charter schools, they were eager to show that they could also raise achievement in a public school system:

> In most cases, we came to them, giving them the ideas behind our strategic planning and what we wanted in place. They all said, "We don't have any place that's a public school district that looks quite like you. And we would be interested in being a part of [an] entire district [that's] going to offer 100 percent choice . . . a system of small schools that are setting out to all be college bound, etc., etc." So they liked the way we talked. (Morrison)

One of the model developers, Scott Dolquist, who at the time was executive director of Expeditionary Learning Schools, later said:

> I think what really was attractive in the beginning was that there was an openness in the district to really [undertaking] the whole thing, and . . . the notion that doing something in one place would have a big impact in another. And I think that on an intellectual level, that was attractive because clearly here was a district that wasn't just moving the deck chairs around.

As a result of extensive site visits, several whole school reform models emerged as front-runners for implementation in MPS: the Big Picture Company, Expeditionary Learning, Early College High School, New Technology High School, and the Coalition of Essential Schools.[5] While each option had a distinct curricular focus, each represented a constructivist approach to teaching and learning—mirroring the superintendent's and executive team members' own instructional preferences.

MPS leaders insisted on some control over the implementation of each model. One program that was highly regarded by a visiting team was rejected because the developers, committed to teacher leadership, were unwilling to have a school principal. From the district's perspective, having a principal or school director was a nonnegotiable requirement. Yet at the same time, the executive team pledged to maintain a high degree of fidelity to the models:

For each model, that collaboration or discussion over "How should this model be implemented in Mapleton?" has looked a little bit different. Some of the models are more insistent that certain pieces of it stay intact. Other models were able to say, "Yeah, we're a little more open about that, so if this is how you want to make a change, then we can work it this way, and this way, and this way." So there was a pretty good working agreement with all of our partners about how the district would work with them to make it be okay. (Morrison)

During this period, CSSI continued to support Mapleton's planning, funneling more than $150,000 to the district for this purpose. Meanwhile, the model partners also promised significant support, mostly for staff development.

In late fall 2003, the district announced in its newsletter, the *Mapleton Messenger*, that MPS would open the following year with "a system of three college preparatory schools that are smaller by design." The traditional high school program would remain in place for juniors and seniors, but two new options would be offered to freshmen and sophomores:

- An Expeditionary Learning High School would connect "rigorous classroom instruction with hands-on community fieldwork," with a particular focus on "teamwork, reflection, and literacy."

- A Big Picture High School (housed in a separate building), with its motto "one student at a time," would provide personalized learning, support from individual advisers, and community-based internships.

The district promised that, during the first year of the reform, all students would "be part of the Skyview High School system" and "have opportunities to participate in a variety of extracurricular activities, including sports, art, music and special clubs, choices not normally offered in a charter or private school environment." The statement continued:

The aim of these "Small by Design" initiatives is to raise expectations, improve student learning and prepare students for success after graduation. Each student will be held to the same academic rigor, regardless of the option they choose, by meeting or exceeding established district and state graduation requirements and standards, including CSAP and ACT tests. All students will graduate earning a Skyview High School diploma.

Implementing the whole school reform models would require major changes in curriculum and instruction. With their emphasis on inquiry- and project-based learning, the models would place enormous demands on students, teachers, and administrators—all at a time when the state was demanding higher CSAP scores and adherence to state curriculum standards. While adoption of these nontraditional approaches increased the political risks of reinventing MPS, the school board, the superintendent, her executive team, and key administrators felt that only a reform of this kind could break the cycle of low expectations and poor achievement.

In order for the promise of the models to be realized, they had to be fully and successfully implemented. The scope of the task, and the political and logistical challenges, were huge:

- Full conversion would mean dismantling the existing high school. Skyview High, with its strong athletic and musical traditions, was beloved by those who had grown up in Mapleton. Would the community accept its elimination?

- In operating a network of small high schools, the district would confront issues involving transportation, food services, scheduling, transcripts and course credits, and extracurricular activities such as sports and band. Would classified staff address these issues successfully?

- Teachers would have to apply for jobs in the new small schools, and the configurations of their jobs would change. Would the union allow this?

- Teachers wanting to remain in the district would have to be trained in constructivist pedagogy. There would be radical changes in the areas of curriculum, lesson planning, and discipline. Would teachers stand for this?

- Project-based learning increases students' responsibility for their learning, requiring them to take the initiative in determining what they have to learn in order to succeed. Would students rise to the challenge?

- Continuing negotiations with model developers would pit model fidelity against district accountability. To what extent would promoters of the various models tolerate this?

In short, implementation of this extensive high school reform would leave no standard operating procedure untouched. Could it really be done? Some MPS leaders may have had doubts, but to keep the reform momentum going, they did not express them publicly.

MOBILIZING FOR DISTRICTWIDE REFORM

Charlotte Ciancio was a novice superintendent when she assumed leadership of the Mapleton Public Schools in 2001, yet she began her tenure with ambitious goals. She was determined to improve low-performing schools by raising everyone's expectations about what Mapleton students could achieve, and by re-creating that sense of family pervasive in the district when she and many other current Mapleton staff were growing up. She believed in the Gates Foundation's mantra of rigor, relevance, and relationships, and, after exploring alternatives, became convinced that small schools and constructivist approaches together would improve achievement, increase graduation rates, and provide students with hope for their future.

Most reform-minded superintendents start their reforms at the elementary level. Elementary schools are smaller and less compartmentalized than high schools; teachers tend to be less entrenched and have less departmental or disciplinary turf to protect. Moreover, younger children's test scores tend to be more malleable—more responsive to reforms—than the scores of high school students.

Ciancio and the school board, however, made a pragmatic decision to begin their reform effort at the secondary level. The idea of high school reform was not new to Mapleton: teachers had proposed (but never implemented) a plan to create a CES-style small school within Skyview. Thus, Ciancio and the school board knew they could draw on a cadre of teachers who had been interested in this type of reform since the 1980s.

The overriding reason for focusing on the high schools, however, was the poor and ever-declining test scores. The state's testing program, CSAP, increased the stakes by magnifying the publicity and the consequences associated with poorly performing schools. Meanwhile, high school enrollment was slipping, as parents concerned about low academic performance and behavior issues at Skyview began sending their children elsewhere.

Many urban superintendents keep a closed circle of advisers as they develop a mission for a district. Then, once the mission has been put into words, they garner support from key constituencies inside and outside the schools. In contrast, Ciancio mobilized the school board, stakeholders in the school community, funders, union leadership, and state officials to embrace the vision of inventing a network of small schools that offered curricular choice and met the learning needs of a variety of students.

From the earliest stages of the planning process, Ciancio was already thinking about strategies to bring a wide range of stakeholders on board for that vision. The 2002 strategic planning process in Estes Park involved community and business people, teachers, staff, and other stakeholders. In spite of the vulnerability Ciancio felt in opening the process to so many, she came to recognize the political capital she gained in doing so. Ciancio recalls meeting with the facilitator, Bill Cook, at the end of the first day, to express her concerns:

> I said, "I am so afraid of what this is going to look like, and what if it comes out and I'm not going to be able to do it? What if we come up with some kind of a system I can't support?" [Cook] pushed himself up from the table and he said, "Charlotte, a strategic plan is intended

to free you to lead. It gives you permission to fulfill the mission that's created by a team. So there's no reason to be afraid of the process—you have to invest in the process . . . If you come into this with a decision about what you want, you'll never be able to lead because you won't have been granted that permission by those that must follow."

I think about him a lot. The grounding and understanding that the strategic plan provided really has freed us to lead, because it has given us permission to move forward.

Ciancio and others believe that without the broad participation of stakeholders from the very beginning, the reform could not have succeeded:

Everyone left feeling like they contributed. Everyone believed in what we said we wanted to do. There was a lot of debate on that day. The union president was there. And he and I didn't necessarily agree on the approach to things. He was pushing a very unique union manner, and I was pushing kind of a management approach to it. And we both had to come to the middle on that, and we had to agree. And it worked . . .

I think if anyone is going to have any type of real success in reform, they have to plan strategically like that. And it's not just long-term, long-range planning . . . You're getting down to what your values are. You are grounding your work in your value system. The other plans will all come later, but if you don't get clear on what you value as a community, you can't move forward.

Executive team members still talk about the importance of developing the mission statement and keeping it at the forefront of the district's efforts:

It really is about, "What is your mission?" And if you don't know what that is, then that's your first step . . . to build a mission or a vision for what you want, and make sure that you have an audience and support staff that believe in that mission.

The mission is probably the most important thing. Every time we visit someone or somebody comes and visits us, they go, "OK, the mission . . ." and then, "How did you put three schools in a build-ing?" I know that our mission has kept us on the right track. And it's somebody's job, or many people's job, to bring that mission back to life if they see it fading. (Masterson)

Ciancio's vision depended heavily on broad parent support and neighborhood backing of the small school reform. In early 2003, as de-tails of the strategic plan began to fill in, she initiated five community meetings around the district, which were attended by twelve hundred parents. At those meetings, board members presented the small school plan. They explained that every high school student would have to ap-ply to one of the three high schools the following year, and that students would be transported around the district to their schools of choice. Not all of the parents welcomed these changes, however, and about one hundred families left the district the following year.

Meanwhile, the executive team divided constituencies between them, with each member meeting with selected individuals or groups to explain the vision and strategy. One member spoke with school sec-retaries, another with custodial staff. A third spoke with community partners, including police and fire departments, the Rotary Club, and others. Of course, members also spoke with teachers. The district devel-oped sophisticated media materials to explain and promote the strategic plan, and specifically the conversion to small schools.

Ciancio's efforts to gain community support for the reform paid off handsomely. There was relatively little public criticism of the closing of Skyview and the importation of whole school reform models from other cities. In addition, Ciancio instituted the reform in a way that shielded it (at least initially) from NCLB sanctions. Beginning in 2003, high schools became subject to NCLB requirements. Ciancio knew that Skyview (and most of the district's other schools) would fail to achieve what the law defined as Adequate Yearly Progress. But the small schools that replaced Skyview were considered "new schools" and therefore exempted from regular reporting requirements for their first two years. CSAP scores for 2005 would become the baseline from which to measure their perfor-mance. Moreover, by closing Skyview High School and opening several small schools in its place, each with new staff and grade configurations, she preempted the state by doing what it would have done in response to poor test performance. In these ways, Ciancio bought time for the re-invention of the district, since the small schools would not be expected to show gains until the third year of implementation.

Although school choice was a fundamental principle of the reform, the whole school reform models all shared a single pedagogical orientation: student-centered, constructivist instruction. Constructivist methods are project based and inquiry oriented. They proceed from the notion that genuine learning occurs only when students wrestle with problems that are meaningful to them. Teachers work closely with students, developing relationships that enable them to link new material to students' interests. For this reason, constructivism is a natural choice for school models that emphasize relevance, or the connection between subject matter, students' interests, and real-world issues.

While constructivist methods have gained in popularity over the past twenty years, however, research findings on their effectiveness are inconclusive. Like the small schools research, research on constructivist pedagogy is based largely on case studies that do not control for critical key variables. For this reason, it is difficult for researchers to attribute gains or losses in achievement specifically to constructivist methods.

To be fair, challenges of this kind are faced by researchers seeking to validate any educational approach. The factors that influence teaching and learning are complex and interrelated, often making it impossible to determine the causes of different outcomes.[6] In addition, public school structure, scheduling, and policies place tremendous constraints on research designs. Features critical to experimental designs, such as random sampling of students, uniform delivery of the method being researched, and equal distribution of students by income level, ethnicity, and achievement level, are generally impossible to implement.[7]

That said, the research-based evidence that any kind of pedagogy leads to academic gains as measured by test scores is weak.[8] Effectively delivered constructivist instruction cannot be shown to be superior to effectively delivered traditional instruction.[9] Nevertheless, district leaders and many Mapleton teachers were convinced that the most assured way to boost student achievement is to build genuine relationships between students and staff and to offer students a curriculum that they find meaningful and relevant to their lives. A reform along these lines would, they believed, keep students in school and increase their engagement with learning, which in turn would lead to improved graduation rates and higher test scores. It was a compelling logic model, even if it wasn't a proven formula.

Ciancio believed deeply in this model—and she wasn't alone. Hired with strong support from her board, she stepped into the superintendency surrounded by an administrative team with whom she had strong philosophical affinities as well as personal and professional ties. In fact, she had applied for the position only because she knew that several of her former colleagues—including some who had been her classmates when she was growing up—would be working closely with her at the district office. All of these educators were committed to small school reform, constructivist pedagogy, and the creation of a system that would allow students "to pursue their interests and gifts." They shared the vision, resolve, and trust required to embark on a major reform. Yet they could not envision all the dilemmas they would face as they instituted small schools in Mapleton.

CHAPTER THREE

Reinventing a District

Implementing Small School Reform

By the summer of 2003, Mapleton had formulated a plan for opening several small schools that would, taken together, offer the "enticing
menu of learning opportunities" called for in the mission and strategic plan. District leaders had won support for the plan from the school
board, parents, and other community members. And this support, in
turn, was essential in obtaining the blessing of the Colorado Department of Education (CDE).

Although it was not obvious to many, the reform depended on a solid
partnership with CDE. Mapleton's test scores were among the lowest
in the state. CDE was pressuring the district to improve student performance and was prepared to impose sanctions if it failed to do so.
Mapleton administrators were no less determined to see scores go up,
but they didn't know how quickly the reforms might generate improvement. Only by working collaboratively with CDE would the district be
able to implement its reforms unfettered by potential sanctions.

Charlotte Ciancio captured the relationship between Mapleton and
CDE when she said: "CDE can't be your adversaries, because they'll
win. It's really the same lesson as the schools. If the schools see the
school district as the adversaries, they lose. So it's all the way up the
pipeline. You need those people who 'supervise' you, so to speak,

because they are the ones who have the authority to take your privileges away."

CDE staff found Mapleton's commitment and vision compelling, and they gave the district's leaders space to implement the reforms without placing demands that might have distracted them from the effort. The CDE accreditation officer explained:

> Mapleton, among all the metro districts, was one of the three or four worst performing . . . And we said, "We're really concerned, and you've got to improve." Well, unlike many districts that you send these letters to, instead of push[ing] back, that district just said, "You're right. We're lousy. We aren't serving our kids well." This was the board and the superintendent, Charlotte, at that point. "We have got to reinvent this place and revamp the whole thing, and do it in a way that will really make a difference for our kids, because we're not doing the job . . ." And we down here were kind of shocked with that, at first. It was like, "Wow, what is this? We haven't seen anything like this."
>
> So for two years now, I have gone around the state in my normal duties, talking about Mapleton as the model of the most significant reform in the state of Colorado. And that puts a lot of burden on them. But it also explains why we have never moved to add more penalties to them. (Phillips, 2006)

The superintendent provided the inspiration, single-mindedness, and daring to launch the reform, and the executive team added its educational, managerial, and financial expertise. Ciancio had assembled a team that was fiercely loyal to her and to the vision. Its members were also comfortable and direct with one another. Nearly all of them had worked in Mapleton since the 1980s, in a variety of capacities. They understood the district's history, culture, community, and prior experiences with reform. Some had waited decades for the chance to create a system of small schools.

In January 2004, the school board approved a plan to open two new small schools the following August. Given all that had to be done with respect to facilities, staffing, and logistics, this was quite a short timeline. Yet there were several reasons for moving ahead quickly.

First, the executive team feared that a cautious, incremental reform would get bogged down in bureaucratic issues, and consequently lose both momentum and community support. Second, they recognized that the district was at risk of losing its state accreditation because of low test scores, and they were eager to show state officials their sincere intention to put their vision into action. One member summed up the executive team's views:

> Here's this young, fledgling reform effort that we're trying to roll out. If we pamper it too long, someone else is going to come in and say, "Your district isn't accredited. Your scores aren't high enough. We're going to bring our own people in." And then we felt like that was going to squash the movement . . . So we had a leverage point of the state being interested in us doing something different . . . but the window of opportunity was small. So we just collectively, including myself, decided that we would take some hits. (Masterson)

Finally, district leaders wanted to act before any changes in the makeup of the school board cost them critical support. In Mapleton, school board elections occur every other year. With each election cycle, three of the five board members go before the voters. As one state school board official explained, "The critical piece in this whole thing is to keep the school board unified in the vision." Other Colorado districts had been stymied in their reform efforts when their board membership changed.

The benefits of moving quickly, however, were accompanied by risks. First, teachers and administrators might become frustrated by the many changes coming at them at once. This happened. Second, support for the reform could be threatened by uncoordinated or poor communication about plans, policies, or procedures from the central office to school administrators, teachers, students, and parents. This happened, too. Finally, the reform could be undermined by logistical failures in areas such as transportation. This nearly happened. That it didn't is a reflection of the earnest efforts by stakeholders at all levels of the system.

Managing the logistics in ways that honored the vision may be the very essence of the Mapleton reform story. Over the course of several months, the district would have to bring two new high schools on line while supporting the traditional high school in its final year. During the next two years, additional high schools would be created, even while the district planned similar transformations of ten elementary and middle schools throughout the district.

Logistics refers to the complex infrastructure that enables a district to function day to day. Changes in logistics can disrupt district operations and crash a reform—especially a reform as complex and far-reaching as the one Mapleton envisioned. Maintaining fidelity to the models, hiring teachers capable of applying the constructivist methods those models called for, balancing district control and school autonomy—all of these disrupted standard operating procedures related to budgeting, hiring, transportation, food services, extracurricular programs, and other common activities in the life of the district.

Because Mapleton was the first district in the country to implement choice for all of its high school students, there were no blueprints on how to conduct such a reform. In the following sections, we provide brief overviews of a few considerations that arose as Mapleton implemented its plan. In doing so, we hope to convey the massive restructuring required to dismantle the existing structures and create a network of small schools.

ADOPTING A CONSTRUCTIVIST PARADIGM

As we have seen, Mapleton's superintendent and executive team favored student-centered and constructivist classroom approaches.[1] Thus, in the small school classrooms, students would be working by themselves or in small groups, investigating, analyzing, testing, exploring, discussing, and applying math, science, or social studies concepts to solve authentic problems. Daily and weekly lessons would revolve around interdisciplinary activities and projects, often involving internships, expeditions, or other types of fieldwork, and not around whole-group instruction, lectures, or traditional content-area textbooks and handouts.

One school director described several characteristics associated specifically with the Big Picture school:

One adviser stays with a group or a cadre of students for all four years of high school, and that one adviser is the primary organizer of all academic subject areas for those students. So students don't have classes.[2] They don't use textbooks—unless, on an individual basis, they're interested in a textbook . . .

Every teacher, every adviser working with their colleagues, creates their own schedule, so kids are not doing the same thing all the time, so therefore there are no bells. We don't give grades. Students are evaluated using primarily an internship process, and also constant dialogue and assessment between the adviser and the student and the student's mentor. So along the way the goal is that every student who's enrolled here will have an outside-of-the-school-building internship experience during every year that they're here . . . And a big part of our job as a school is to help students discover what things they might be interested in, because often they come with fairly limited perspectives about what they could be interested in.

An administrator of the Welby New Technology High School described his school's approach this way:

All the curriculum that we do here is project-based learning. So it makes a much more relevant match to the kids. A quick example: when I was a freshman in high school, I learned mean, median, mode, averages by doing fifty problems of each and turning those problems in on a worksheet at the end of the day. Here, kids learn those same mathematical concepts through a project where they're asked to analyze five different cell phone plans, add in the start-up costs, the overage charges, the cost per minute, and figure out the mean, median, mode, and average cost per minute. And what they do with that information is create graphs, get an understanding of why it's important to know those concepts, and present that data to . . . a panel comprised of outside business people or parents, to demonstrate which is the best cell phone plan and why. And so, with that, not only are they learning those mathematical skills, they're also learning oral presentation . . . They're reading technical literature, technical writing, to understand the contracts and things like that.

However strong the district's commitment to constructivist methods, most Mapleton teachers were not initially trained in this approach, nor had they experienced this mode of teaching as students. Furthermore, as implementation began, 70 percent of Mapleton's teachers had been teaching for five years or less. During the first two years of the reform (2004–05 and 2005–06), coaches from the model partners—including Big Picture Company, Expeditionary Learning, and New Technology—worked with school leaders and staff to help them adopt the models' instructional practices. At Skyview Academy, which was based on CES principles but had no model partner, assistance came from mentors within the district.

External Partners and Model Fidelity

Although the model partners (with the exception of International Baccalaureate, a later addition) were similar in their instructional philosophies, they did not always view the replication process, or their role in the Mapleton district, in the same way. Scott Dolquist, former executive director of Expeditionary Learning Schools, offered one perspective:

> The real challenge is, how does an outside partner make sure that there's fidelity to what they had in mind, as opposed to having it all twisted around by what the district needs? . . . I think that for everybody that is involved in this, that becomes an immediate source of tension. And for those people who are really intent on implementing any model, it just is a constant worry . . . "If I don't pay attention to this and I don't keep it on my plate, the work that we're doing will just become like any other program we've all seen in education: a few people do some stuff for a while and then it just goes away." I think sustainability and fidelity are really tricky, and I certainly don't think we've got it all figured out yet.

Dolquist embarked on the relationship with Mapleton with the intention of maintaining a long-term commitment to Expeditionary Learning (EL) schools in the district:

> We made an early decision that, if the Gates people would let us, we would play this out for at least five years. I think that this is

essential . . . If we hadn't done that, this would have been a disaster, and it wouldn't have been an EL school. We could have been in that situation where we would have said, "You can't even call it an EL school," because we wouldn't have been able to be with them for a long enough period of time.

Dolquist's views were shaped by the track record of comprehensive school reform grants, which typically last just three years. "Most of that stuff is not around today," he said, "because a three-year format never guarantees that something is really going to be in place."

Let's just play out the high school part. Let's say you just had ninth-grade teachers [in a school's first year], and then the next year you'd have ninth and tenth, then ninth, tenth, eleventh, then ninth, tenth, eleventh, twelfth. It would be five years—a planning year plus four years—where you'd still have brand-new teachers coming into the model in the fifth year. And so, those teachers would have barely had any training from us. The ideal scenario is, once the grant is over, the school would be an EL school, and that district . . . or the school would continue to partner with us.

Dolquist acknowledges that EL can't expect schools to pay for extensive mentoring, to the tune of $60,000 to $70,000 a year, forever. So the question becomes: What will the relationship between an EL school and the model partner look like six or seven years after start-up? "Does it look like you're a member with us with a little support for a year, and then you come back with a larger contract as you get new teachers? Do you need to reengage with us? I don't know that we've figured it out right yet. Does the problem exist? Absolutely."

If he were starting over again in Mapleton, Dolquist said, he would spend more time at the beginning talking specifically about the structures and expectations of EL schools. "Although we talked about fidelity to the Expeditionary Learning model, I don't think we were clear enough about what that looked like, and what that really meant," he explained. As a result, there were points during implementation when EL was "pushing the envelope" in ways that the district had not envisioned:

I'm not sure that our memo of understanding spoke to [requirements of the model] clearly enough. We were very clear about the school having enough autonomy to implement the model, and everybody nodded their heads. But I'm not sure we were all clear enough about, "And what this means is . . . " So I think that the devil is in the details, to some degree. But also it's an awkward relationship. I don't mean with Mapleton, I just mean in general . . . I don't think that I have brilliant insights yet about this, except to say that when you find the right building-level leaders and the right people from the model who are working there, they tend to forge a good enough relationship that they kind of make it work.

Elliott Washor, codirector of the Big Picture Company, offers another perspective on school reform. He believes that autonomy is necessarily limited:

You don't walk in thinking that you're going to be left alone. In public schools, there's all kinds of accountability—parents, school boards, teachers, kids . . . Utopia is not an option. And it wasn't an option ever at the Met in Providence [the flagship Big Picture school]. There are always compromises to your ideals and theories. And that's why I like [us] to think of ourselves as practitioners—as a practice, not a philosophy. And so I go in thinking that way, and thinking that I'm willing to make those compromises. As long as we feel we are creating schools that are successful for students and staff, we're happy.

Washor insists that what he brings to a district is a *design*, not a model, and that the design will inevitably be shaped by the environment in which it is implemented:

When you look at a design, it's based on the needs of the people who use it. And [that] creates flexibility, whereas a model, to me, has a lot more rigidity to it. I hear that word "model" a lot, and I cringe. You have to adapt to your local environment. You have to adapt to your people. We were not as clear at the beginning as we are now about these things . . . It's supposed to evolve and be flexible. It can't stay the same; it just can't. The conditions are changing so much. Our world is changing. We have to adapt to it or else we're dead.

In our interview, Washor cited Starbucks as an illustration of flexible design. "To me," he said, "no two Starbucks are the same."

> You ever go to a Starbucks in New Orleans? Ever go to a Starbucks in New York? You watch the difference in how the people in the Starbucks in New Orleans [talk to the customers]. "Wait a second . . . do you want to try this first before you buy? Let me give you a little bit." You know: "How about a little more sugar, sugar?" I mean, that's what it's like. But it's still Starbucks. But the people make it a little different.

Because Washor expects that Big Picture schools will continually adapt to each district's needs and conditions, he is less concerned than Dolquist is about initial clarity surrounding details of the model. Whereas Dolquist advises model partners and school districts to articulate exactly what each model demands, Washor's approach is to rely on general understandings about the Big Picture design and goals. He doesn't believe that carefully articulated contracts are always helpful:

> When it comes down to it, when the people change, the papers mean nothing. Meanwhile, a new superintendent comes and she says, "I didn't sign this agreement." The contract creates inflexibility a lot of times, and things have to change. I say, "Sure, if you're going to have a contract on paper, make it thin." So we have a two-page memo of understanding, knowing that they aren't our schools and we can get kicked out any time.
>
> But even if we were a charter management organization, the way the state's changing policy all the time—No Child Left Behind and all this other stuff—there's no guarantees that you're going to stick around because you have a big long contract that you mulled over for a year and a half. [We] say, "Wait a second, it says so right here," and [district administrators] go, "Too bad." I've watched that happen. The contract says [the model partner] selects [the principal], and the

superintendent comes through and says, "Here's your new principal." We make the decision to leave, or they make the decision to get rid of us. All of that is part and parcel of what a school developer faces.

In lieu of detailed contracts, Washor relies on good working relationships with the people involved:

> You're dealing with people, and people create the system . . . Now, some people out there and in our own organization have their own vision for what this should look like. And so they are the ones, a lot of times, that don't want to compromise certain things. And they argue it out then, which isn't a bad thing—this is still a democracy . . . I don't mind a good argument and people changing their minds and opinions.

We asked Washor whether there were core design principles that can't be sacrificed if a school is to remain a Big Picture school: "Well, look: nobody has schools our size. Even if we went to 200, nobody could match that, even—let alone staying at 150, 160. Nobody has schools where you have an adviser for four years. Nobody has schools where they are out two days a week developing their interests."

Above all, Washor says, a visitor can identify a Big Picture school by listening to what students say about it: "If they articulate about courses, rather than about getting self-actualized about who they are, then you know it's not a Big Picture school anymore."

Charlotte Ciancio shares Washor's views on the question of "model" versus "design": "I would say that [model partners] need to understand that their model is a design, it's truly a design, and that they need to take their philosophy and the mission of their work and design it in the context of a new community. So I would encourage them to be flexible, stay nimble as they work through the issues."

For its part, Ciancio says, Mapleton never wanted to create mere replicas of the schools that the planning teams had visited, "because we didn't have the same children they did. And we are a community that is unique, as I believe every community is. So we had the sole intention of taking the principles of their work and the really solid research-based experiences they had had, and applying it in our context." Hence the dilemma: how faithful should the district be to each reform model?

Ciancio now believes that, in early discussions with the model partners, she and her executive team were not "as explicit or as articulate" as they could have been about the manner in which they would be changing the designs. This reticence, she says, made it difficult to push back later on: "So, if I were to do it again, I'd have exposed our skill and exposed our intellect more quickly than I did. We took a really humble approach, and I don't think that served us well."

In spite of challenges surrounding model fidelity, Ciancio believes that the district's collaborations with model partners were valuable:

> We'd definitely still enter into [relationships with model partners], because they really do scaffold your school district. They were willing to bring expertise and resources that we didn't have without them. So I still think they were incredibly valuable . . . The network to which we're now connected is so much broader and so much stronger than it would have been without them. So I would do it again.

Dolquist, Washor, and Ciancio each speak of the importance of establishing good working relationships. As the reform progressed, the professional relationships that had formed among educators early on were critical to overcoming obstacles as they arose. Ciancio noted: "If you have a strong relationship with your partners, you can tackle just about anything. So, it's really important not to be afraid of developing that relationship and really depending on one another and really trusting one another's skill set."

Hiring School Leaders

The choice of who would lead the new small schools was crucial. In Mapleton, the leadership role in each school is assumed by a "director," not a "principal." Directors are expected to display an entrepreneurial spirit. They assemble a staff of teachers who share their vision of what the school is to be and guide them in realizing that vision. They are also responsible for explaining and promoting the school to students, parents, and the wider community.

School directors were expected to lead in a manner that incorporated democratic, inclusive processes. The rationale was simple: if the directors wanted their teachers to give students choices, foster independent thinking, inquisitiveness, and exploration, and acknowledge that no one had all the answers, they needed to adopt a leadership style that modeled those practices. As one school director explained:

> Collaboration as a learning outcome for students is also one for us as staff. Collaboration is something we hold in high regard here, and shared leadership and shared decision making. That's been part of, I'd say, my personal/professional evolution . . . It's kind of a paradigm shift, from what can be efficient and get to the next task compared to what is probably best for the teachers and students. (Simons)

The executive team recruited directors who valued this type of leadership. Some directors (typically those hired from outside the district) came with the necessary qualities, while others (typically those hired from within the district) learned them on the job.

In some cases, the model partners participated in the selection of school directors. When Mapleton Expeditionary School for the Arts (MESA), the second of two Expeditionary Learning high schools, opened in Mapleton, EL worked out an arrangement with the district so that EL representatives (including Dolquist) sat on the hiring committee. Only candidates approved by the entire committee would be forwarded to the superintendent, who made the final hiring decision. Dolquist said:

> Although it had its hard moments, we really did insist on helping to pick the leader. Although that was tricky, and I think hard, I think it was the right decision, and I think that the person who is there is the right start-up person for MESA . . . But what kind of worked is that a person's name wouldn't even get to [the superintendent] unless we had agreed that [candidates] were acceptable to the people in the district and to EL . . . I think that honored [the fact] that ultimately we

were not paying the salaries of those people and yet we were the ones that felt responsible for implementing the model.

The hiring of teachers for the EL schools worked similarly, with EL staff participating. Dolquist said that this provided a good balance between director control and model input. "Ultimately, it would be the principal's decision. But I think the insights that our staff provided [were helpful], because they have more experience than a fairly young principal. But also, they were used to the model, which was really critical to the hiring process. I think that was all really quite good."

Hiring Teachers

School directors were allowed a great deal of latitude in the teacher hiring process, and the procedures for interviewing and selecting teachers were not customary ones. The district's traditional hiring policy gave priority to Mapleton teachers when a new school or new program opened, and it honored existing contractual stipulations regarding pay, teaching responsibilities, and professional development. Under the new procedures, however, teachers from outside the district were given equal status with Mapleton veterans. Current teachers were not guaranteed a position in the small schools or, if hired, a position in their area of expertise.

Thus, Mapleton teachers had to interview for the new positions, and in order to work in the small schools they had to accept requirements that were not part of their existing contracts. For example, the small schools required group planning time but reduced the planning time allowed to individual teachers. The school day was extended, and teachers were expected to work twenty extra days for credit but no pay.

Yet the teachers union, far from putting up roadblocks to the reform, actually became a partner with the administration in advocating for it. The union approved addenda to existing teacher contracts, accepting new job requirements that would remain in effect until the contracts were renegotiated up to three years later.

Why was the union so accommodating? One reason was that union leaders personally believed in the reform. One union leader explains:

[T]his union has a pretty good working relationship with the central administration . . . We weren't adversarial to begin with. Personally, I believed in the change, in the small school concept. So for me as a leader, I tried to impart that to the rest of my leadership. Now, did everybody agree? No. There was lots of fighting. But for me personally, I thought this was a way we needed to go. So . . . what can we do with the [contract] language to make sure that teachers are still protected and to make sure that this reinvention can go forward? (Strum)

The reform was attractive to many teachers, who were promised a great deal of control in the design and governance of their schools. This is reflected in our interview with the head of the teachers union:

UNION LEADER: For the first time, teachers had the chance to become empowered in the decision making and running. And I don't care if you're running a vegetable stand, if you're giving your employee the power and voice in which to have a meaningful part in that, you're going to get 150 percent buy-in. Sure you're going to have a few hesitant people that aren't going to be on board. But at the same time, that helps to get the buy-in from a union standpoint.

INTERVIEWER: You said you weren't popular for a while?

UNION LEADER: I would say, basically, because we all hate change and tradition is much more common to us. But you have to reinvent the wheel, otherwise we'd still be on stone wheels.

Just as district leaders sought directors committed to the goals of the reform, school directors sought teachers who fully understood the models and were dedicated to putting them into practice. Such teachers would embrace a school culture that emphasized collaborative decision making and constructivist pedagogy. As a former Mapleton superintendent observed, directors of the new small schools couldn't "just go out and do job fairs and get any teacher. Not any teacher is going to be able to do this."

Each director developed a way of presenting the school's values and goals to teacher candidates. One director prepared a list of philosophical beliefs and professional development expectations and required candidates to sign it before he would review their applications. "They would read the list and many would say, 'Well, that's not quite for me.' So they would self-select." (Kensington) The director needed Ciancio's support to adopt this screening process, but she was solidly behind him.

Another director placed a premium on commitment to students, content knowledge, and collegiality:

There were three things that I talked about a lot in the interview process . . . To be successful here, I thought you had to, first of all, love kids—and you had to love kids that you knew were going to come with challenges. You had to love content, because our model requires that teachers do a lot of their own curriculum design around certain content areas. So you have to like—really like—digging into the Harlem Renaissance yourself as a learner, to be able to put together that curriculum for students. And the third was that you really had to be committed to and enjoy working with colleagues . . . [W]e have so much collaboration that we do as a matter of course, with our grade-level teams and the way that planning is done, that you couldn't really be a lone ranger who likes to lock [yourself] in [your] own room and do that work. (Lewis)

Another school director emphasized teachers' adaptability and resilience:

[T]he person has got to be a generalist. So, even though [you] studied language arts in college, you better have taken math, because you've got to be conversant in pretty higher-level math. And we want people who are comfortable supervising instruction in all subject areas. So we're very intentionally looking for bright, bright people who can be flexible across disciplines . . . That's a pretty massive hiring shift. That is, we're not just looking for a social studies teacher. In fact, one of the questions in our interview is, "Are you willing to give up your discipline? . . . OK, you're passionate about World War II. Are you willing to give that up, if that's not what your kids need?" (Taylor)

The hiring process for the new schools did cause stress for many teachers. Teachers had to interview for jobs at specific schools, and they were told there were "no guarantees." Also, the timing was such that some teachers would not hear which schools they would be hired for until late summer—after the hiring season. One teacher explained the process:

> As a faculty member we all had a seniority number that was assigned to us based on the date of our hire . . . We had a few weeks to find out about each of the models. Then we had a deadline where we had to choose our three top choices. So we just choiced into our top three, and then, if your seniority number came up in the time that that position was being filled for that particular school, then [you] got it. And if somebody else was in a high seniority number, they got ahead of us . . . Thirty-five percent was the number of teachers who choiced in and didn't get any of their three top choices. (Yvonne)

Teachers with whom we spoke said that, although the process created anxiety, teachers who stayed were generally pleased with where they ended up. Yet teacher turnover increased after implementation, spiking in 2006–07 to 33 percent of all secondary teachers. This was the year following the closing of the traditional Skyview High School. Many teachers near retirement at the beginning of the reform stayed with Skyview and simply retired when the school closed. Yet the percentage of new hires among Mapleton's teachers remained high in succeeding years: 20 percent in 2008 and 22 percent in 2009, compared with 15 and 8 percent, respectively, in the pre-reform years of 2003 and 2004 (see figure 3.1).[3]

There is no denying that small school reform led to high turnover and cost the district many experienced teachers. As we discuss in chapter 6, the sustainability of the reform will depend in part on whether the district can retain teachers who have been with the reform from the beginning.

FIGURE 3.1 Percentage of new hires at secondary level, 2003–2009

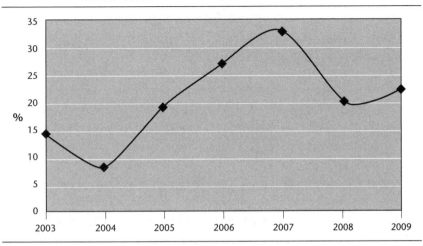

Redesigning Professional Development

With the advent of small schools, professional development assumed a new character: it would now be conducted by school directors, rather than by the district. Signs of this shift had appeared even before the first small schools opened. For example, the director of the Coalition of Essential School started bringing his teachers together during the planning year, while they were all still at Skyview. He would assign them groups of randomly selected students so that they could practice new instructional strategies. These "demonstration groups" led to "hours and hours of painstaking conversation and argument," he recalled. "Getting everybody to a common place wasn't easy. But in the end, it really became one of the most valuable periods of time we ever had."

The teachers union worked hand in hand with the directors to make professional development a success. In addition, each small school received support from a coach who had longstanding experience with its particular model. Coaches were drawn from "mentor schools" across the country. They flew to Mapleton to observe classes and then sat down with teachers to offer feedback and advice. Big Picture funded summer conferences and arranged for directors and lead teachers to visit other schools to examine their instructional approaches.

DISTRICT RESTRUCTURING

Apart from changes at the school level, the Mapleton reform required a significant restructuring of district operations. A network of small schools would need expanded bus transportation, meals served at every site, and new budgeting procedures. Those familiar with the management of school districts will appreciate the time and energy it took to revamp basic services and practices. They will also realize that a breakdown at this level would have jeopardized the entire reform.

At an early stage, Charlotte Ciancio and her executive team recognized the importance of obtaining the support of a highly motivated classified staff. In our interviews, the staff members were unanimous in praising Ciancio for including them in the planning. Here is a typical comment:

> I think she wanted everybody to be aware that you need classified as well as certified [staff] to run a school district . . . Let's face it, Charlotte came from the district. She went to school in this district . . . and then she taught here. She worked in student services here, and then she became superintendent . . . I've worked for probably three [other superintendents]. They wouldn't even talk to you. I mean, they didn't even know who you were. Charlotte knows most everybody. (Connolley)

Transportation: Making Choice Genuine

The transportation system underwent significant reorganization. Some of the changes would have occurred even without the reform; many of Mapleton's major streets were under construction, so existing school bus routes had to be redrawn. But now, instead of having a fleet of Skyview buses all arriving at a single destination, the district would have buses taking students to several different high schools located miles apart. New routes to the small schools had to be devised and tested, the various schedules had to be coordinated, and the district had to make sure that no students were spending an inordinate part of each day on a bus. Whenever a route became longer, so did the work hours of drivers and dispatchers. As the district prepared for the second year, when parents would have the option of sending their children to any of six high schools, it was difficult to anticipate how many children would be on any given bus. To make matters more difficult, drivers on the new and expanded routes would often have to deal with children they did not know.

Countless hours of meetings were required to plan and implement the changes in transportation that the reform demanded. The process took months and included constant adjustments and midcourse corrections. Because of early and ongoing communication between transportation staff and leaders at the district and school levels, many problems were anticipated and ironed out before the buses started running. As issues arose in the first few months—shifting school schedules, the adding and dropping of bus stops—communication with parents became a priority: "We're having sixty and seventy kids on a bus. We had to take everybody. And these long routes . . . It seems like it's so immense. Can we do this? And you know, the key to all that is keeping the communication lines open—letting [the parents] know what was happening." (Buchowski)

The bus drivers say that they quickly developed relationships with students and their families, and that these relationships helped prevent disruptive behaviors from escalating into major problems. By getting to know the students, the drivers spontaneously affirmed a core value of the district's new small schools.

Restructuring Budgeting Procedures

Before the reform, Mapleton had allocated funds based on enrollment projections. Out of these funds, principals had paid for supplies and equipment, building maintenance, teacher training materials, and other operating and special expenses. As the small schools prepared to open, however, the central office introduced plan-based (also known as zero-based) budgeting. Under this system, each school director was required to develop a strategic plan that included objectives for curriculum and staff development, as well as detailed action plans and projected costs for accomplishing the objectives. The district would then decide how much money to allocate to each school, based on the needs identified in the plan.

Plan-based budgeting gave the district a mechanism to foster innovation and encourage school directors and staff to engage in ongoing assessment of programs and practices. Under the plan-based approach, school directors and teachers had to study their achievement data, identify objectives for boosting performance, lay out detailed steps to meet the objectives, and specify what it would all cost. The district's budget director explained:

> It really shook things up and made them really look at data. They had to demonstrate from their CSAP data and other data that they were really tackling with resources the biggest identifiable problems in their building. And they would have to come and present it to the executive team and say, "Here's where I'm putting my resources, because we saw that our scores were dropping and we wanted to implement this program . . . " They would have reasons why they would do that and they would present that to us, and then we would fund their program. (Henley)

The budget director believed that the plan-based system helped school directors and staff better understand the broad implications of various instructional decisions:

> A lot of times, especially in here with the people we're working with, they like to be big-picture thinkers, you know, and think of big plans. The plan-based model forces them to put it down on a piece of paper and say, "All right, here's what it's going to take." And then when they bring it to us, [we can] point out, "If [two schools] are really going to start at two different times, that's going to need some different drop-offs. And have you considered the cost of bus routes?"

Oftentimes, we can bring it back to some cost savings that they don't necessarily consider. (Henley)

In addition, plan-based budgeting placed a premium on creative problem solving—precisely the type of innovative thinking that the district wanted to foster.

Nonetheless, Ciancio and the executive team soon realized that the approach had drawbacks. First of all, it led to unequal funding for schools. Under the old system, schools with similar enrollments received the same amount of money. Now, each school's budget was based on its strategic plan, not on the number of students enrolled. Some schools had more than twice the enrollment of others, but their budgets did not necessarily reflect this.

In addition to distorting allocations of resources, the plan-based model was cumbersome for the district's budget staff:

A plan-based model takes a lot of time, and timing of the plan-based model doesn't work real well with the timing I have to work under . . . The latest I can get their budgets from [school directors] is the first week of April. [But] they're not nearly done with their strategic planning by April 2 each year. So what I would usually wind up doing is, I would put in a starter budget for them, and the board would approve that. Then in October, when the pupil count was finalized, we would do a supplemental budget [that] would take into account all their strategic planning, and then I would adjust the budget at that time to match. So, it was awkward and it took a lot more time. (Henley)

The budget director believes that as schools were first defining their goals and strategies, this was time well spent. Once the initial planning process was complete, however, the value of the extra effort diminished. After three years of plan-based budgeting, Mapleton decided to return to an allocation model, but with certain modifications. Under the hybrid approach that the district adopted in 2007, schools are funded according to a formula that takes into account enrollment, teacher experience (which affects professional development needs), percentage of students who are English language learners, percentage of students eligible for free or reduced-price lunch, and other factors. This approach allows school directors to move funding across some line items. If, for example, they want to schedule a late start on a professional development day (so that faculty meet in the morning and students arrive in the afternoon), they can shift funds to cover the necessary costs, such as transportation.

Since creating its system of choice, Mapleton has incurred increased operating expenses. A district with many small schools sacrifices economies of scale. Before the reform, Skyview High School served fourteen hundred students. It had one principal, two assistant principals, one library, one cafeteria, and so on. Multiple schools require multiple directors, libraries, and separate facilities for food services—all paid for out of the same funding source, the state's per-pupil allocation (PPA).

Transportation incurred the biggest costs associated with the reform:

> I knew it was going to go up because of the change of providing transportation to anybody who lived more than a mile away from their school of choice. It was easy before, when you had neighborhood schools with a feeder pattern . . . Johnny lives here, so he's going to Monterey because that's in his area, and he lives right across the street, so no transportation—all done. Well, suddenly with this change, he may choose to go to Valley View. Well, he lives more than one mile from Valley View, and suddenly we have to transport a kid that we didn't have to before. So, total shake-up on just everything to do with transportation, so it's gone up a lot. I just had no way of knowing how much that was going to be. (Henley)

The district launched the reform with a budget surplus of $10 million. By the start of the fourth year of implementation, the surplus had dropped to about $4.5 million. By the fifth year, it was gone. The disappearance of the surplus is partly attributable to the small school reform (see chapter 6 for details).

Making Provisions for Extracurricular Activities

Small school advocates acknowledge that they cannot duplicate the extensive course offerings and extracurricular activities that are often

available in comprehensive high schools. Small schools operate with reduced staff. They adopt a theme-based mission and devote their limited
resources to activities that contribute to the mission. This often means severely limiting extracurricular activities. To proponents of small schools,
the trade-off is justified. They argue that the benefits of personalization
and innovation in a small school outweigh the value of the broad menu
of extracurricular programs offered in traditional high schools. This
argument, however, may underestimate the importance of athletics,
music, and other activities to students and parents who live in the communities affected by small school conversions.

The impact of Mapleton's reform on students' extracurricular participation has been significant. Before the reform, two-thirds of Mapleton's
students engaged in extracurricular activities (about thirty-eight hundred students). By spring 2008, the proportion had fallen to one-third
(about seventeen hundred students).[4] During the course of the reform,
several activities were cut and others disappeared because there wasn't
a critical mass of students in any particular school who wanted to participate. Remaining programs suffered because of reduced accessibility.
Moreover, once students identified with "their" small school, joining
clubs and teams off campus felt like going to another school where they
didn't feel a connection. Because of this, not all activities have been affected equally. Districtwide programs—especially sports—have suffered
the most, while other, school-based extracurricular activities have more
participation than before the reform.

Prior to the reform, Mapleton's athletic program was on an upswing.
After years of large deficits, the athletic budget was in balance. There
was very little turnover among coaches, and the district was even able
to recruit a Hall of Fame football coach from Iowa. Mapleton's tennis, track, volleyball, basketball, and football teams were competitive
at the state level and a source of community pride. Girls had achieved
higher participation rates than boys, and girls' athletics in Mapleton
had been a model for other districts' athletic programs. Between 2002
and 2004, the proportion of Skyview students participating in sports
had doubled, from 27 to 54 percent. Since the reform began, however,
Mapleton has seen a steep decline in athletic participation. In spring

2008 (the most recent year for which data were available), the figure was 16 percent. Now boys outnumber girls (by about 10 percent) in athletic participation.

It is not difficult to understand why Mapleton's athletic program has been adversely affected by the reform. The program still operates out of the Skyview campus, formerly the site of the traditional high school, which therefore has the best athletic facilities. Students who attend schools elsewhere in the district must travel to Skyview to participate in after-school sports. Although the district provides transportation, the students we interviewed expressed concerns about being late to practices or, worse, missing the bus for away games and having to deal with angry coaches or disappointed teammates. A student told us: "The coaches get all mad if you are late or if you are not dressed. But it's not our fault. The buses are late or not arriving on time. But they say it is our responsibility. They say we could call a parent or someone else to pick us up." (Mary Ellen)

Furthermore, the demands of teaching in the new small schools have made it difficult to recruit and retain coaches:

> I would like to have a woman for our basketball position, you know, but [it's] very difficult to get people today to want to coach. There's a tremendous amount of staff training that has to go on. And then there I am, saying, "By the way, did you want to coach?" I did lose some coaches, because they just said, "I don't know when I can do it, because I have all this training I've got to go through." (Norida)

Initially, students attending small schools at sites other than Skyview found it especially difficult to take part in afterschool sports because the different high schools did not have a common dismissal time. To address this problem, the executive team and the directors agreed in the second year to coordinate the small schools' daily schedules:

> We all agreed that we would finish our school day at the exact same time . . . [At] EL and Big Picture, the directors in both of those schools wanted to go, as I recall, until 4:00, and we [at Skyview] were getting

out at 2:35. So we were going to have an hour and a half of dead time waiting on just a couple of kids. So we got together and we worked very cooperatively. They just said, "So what do you need?" And I said, "I need them to be out at 2:35 or 2:40 at the latest, because we have to get them back over here so they can participate." And we did that. (Norida)

Even though basic logistics have been worked out, small schools present perennial obstacles for districtwide activities. In a comprehensive high school, a lot of recruiting takes place between classes, in the cafeteria, or in common areas before or after school, when coaches or other program sponsors see students who show promise and cajole them into trying out:

You see them in the hallway, and I could say, "Marty, you are coming out for swim team, right?" Because I see you, and it's a face-to-face. I have a relationship with you as one of my athletes on the swim team. And you would say, "Yeah, I'm going to be there." Well, now you have almost every one of the coaches in this building, but the kids [are] not. (Norida)

While participation in athletics has declined, the proportion of students in other extracurricular activities has steadily increased. In 2003–04, for example, student government participation accounted for just 6 percent of extracurricular activity. By 2007–08, that figure had risen to 12 percent. During the same period, the proportion of extracurricular activity devoted to academic clubs rose from 26 to 49 percent. Music programs were especially hard hit at the outset of the reform; the number of participating students fell from about eighty before Year One of implementation to fewer than ten immediately after Year One. By 2008, however, music once again accounted for about 22 percent of all extracurricular activity, matching pre-reform levels.

Statistics from spring 2008 suggest some recovery since 2006 in the level of participation in extracurricular activities, but nothing approaching pre-reform levels. Overall, while the district is still able to field complete football and soccer teams, participation in extracurricular activity has shifted from districtwide to school-level activities.

The executive team and school board are committed to fielding and funding the sports teams and bands that have long represented the district with pride. Small school advocates would argue that the promised benefits of the reform, including increased graduation and college attendance rates, outweigh the diminished participation in districtwide extracurricular activities. But this can be a hard sell to students and their parents. It remains to be seen how extracurricular activities will be managed, whether students who come up entirely in small schools will retain expectations of districtwide activities such as sports, music, and proms, and whether the community will rally around specific schools or call for districtwide activities for their children.

Balancing School Autonomy and District Control

In order to preserve Mapleton's high school football and basketball programs, the small schools, as we have seen, agreed on a common dismissal time—a step they had not envisioned in the first year of the reform. "Autonomy" is often cited as a core principle of the small school movement, and while the term has many different meanings and applications, most small school proponents would say that it includes a school's ability to structure its schedule, set its calendar, design its curriculum, hire teachers, recruit students, and allocate resources in ways that enable it to pursue its distinctive mission.

Within a public school district, however, autonomy to carry out these tasks is rarely absolute. How to strike a balance between autonomy and district control? The decision to coordinate not just the small schools' dismissal times, but also their entire academic calendars, illustrates the dilemmas Mapleton faced.

During the first year of implementation (2004–05), each of the three small high schools had its own calendar, and the variations in their daily schedules were significant. Some schools had late starts, while others had early releases. These conflicting schedules took a toll on support staff and on parents, who might have children enrolled in several different schools. After much debate, the executive team decided to roll out a district calendar, but then allow schools to apply for waivers. This opened up a whole new area of negotiations with school directors:

> This morning we went through all the calendar waivers with the principals, and there were places the district just said no. "We never had late starts before for professional development . . . and when you built your own calendars last year, you all put in a lot of late starts. So guess what? This year, in the district calendar, we're going to put a couple late starts in every month, because you clearly all wanted that. So we're going to keep those." But then we had schools [that] wanted two late starts a week, so we said no: "We'll do one a week for you who want it, and that's the middle ground we're going to land on." So then this morning I heard the principals say, "Well, can we buy back a late start if the issue is money? Can we use part of our money to buy back another last start?" Charlotte said no on that one, simply because two late starts a week is just so hard on the community. The one calendar would never work for the models. Seventeen calendars does not work for our community. (Vogel)

As these and similar decisions accumulated, district sensibilities became incrementally more influential over school policies and practices. We do not claim that this was intentional. We believe, however, that it was inevitable.

In his Year Two report on the Mapleton reform, the district's external evaluator captured the dilemma we are describing when he wrote:

> There is a common tension represented here between the benefits of central control (demanding a minimal level of quality, finding ways to more efficiently use resources, etc.) and the benefits of school-site control (quickly adjusting and making resource decisions to reflect unique and ever-changing needs, a greater feeling of ownership, etc.). Mapleton's leadership has tried to strike the right balance—a balance that clearly has not been found universally pleasing.[5]

While Charlotte Ciancio and the executive team supported the directors' efforts to implement their models faithfully, they also set some limits on the small schools' freedom to innovate. To ensure that students could transfer from one school to another, for example, there had to be some common course offerings. But achieving a degree of consistency across schools was no simple matter. If a school based much of its teaching and learning on internships and interdisciplinary projects, how could it conform to the expectations of Algebra I or English III? "English I" was a misnomer if the projects through which instruction was delivered integrated math, social studies, and science as well as English skills.

Not surprisingly, directors resisted organizing their curricula along traditional lines. But children would transfer not only to other schools in Mapleton, but also to schools elsewhere in the state or country. Colleges would scrutinize transcripts. Small school curricula could not be so distinctive as to ignore these realities. In addition, parents and students from different schools talk, compare experiences, and even compete. So the district could not allow one school to offer opportunities or incentives that were significantly different from what other schools offered.

This is another of the dilemmas that Mapleton had to manage but could not resolve. On the one hand, the reform was based on *choice*, which implied that there would be significant diversity among the small schools. A choice-based system would be a sham if all the schools were essentially the same. On the other hand, if curricular offerings differed substantially between schools, the district might face several unwelcome consequences. Students transferring within or out of Mapleton would experience a lack of continuity. Some of the small schools might attract a disproportionate share of students, leading to lopsided enrollments. Finally, district officials would be unable to ensure that the small schools were providing certain common learning experiences that stakeholders such as CDE demanded. Thus, while providing genuine choice was a core *value* of the reform, keeping school offerings equitable was important to the *stability* of the reform in the years ahead.

One school director came up against this dilemma when he developed an innovative program with a local university:

I did a grant proposal and raised money to recruit some stellar students from [the university] who are young Hispanic boys and girls
who came out of this neighborhood, are very successful, are in college, to come and recruit kids to join our school . . . But then the
district felt like we couldn't just do it for one school, so if one school
did it, then all the schools had to do it. So then the students that I
recruited now went from being our recruiters to being recruiters for
six schools. Those kinds of things, I could have done more easily and
more directly if I were just my own solo flyer. But I think the district
understandably has this feeling [that] these are all our kids and no
one kid gets to do things that the other kids don't get to do. (Lewis)

The challenge of balancing small school autonomy against district
mandates has existed since the onset of the reform. Initially, the district
was willing to give considerable weight to school autonomy. But by the
end of the second year (2005–06), logistical realities and pressures from
the state in response to low CSAP scores began shifting the balance in-
exorably toward centralization.

AUTONOMY AND ACCOUNTABILITY

The focus on autonomy in the small school movement has ambigu-
ous roots. Early research focused on successful small, private schools,
which are often independent of public input and scrutiny. Such schools
are unfettered by state-mandated funding formulas, regulations about
class size and facilities management, unions, and laws regarding staffing. We believe it is unrealistic to expect that a public school could be
unaccountable in a public school context, especially since accountability
for a school's success or failure ultimately rests with the superintendent.
In Mapleton, this state of affairs sometimes frustrated school directors,
who were hired because of their commitment to specific models: "Our
school brings in three and one half million dollars. If I just had that
three and a half million dollars and I could run the school as I chose, I
think that I could make many more mission-driven decisions about allocation of resources than we can make now." (Lewis)

The nation's biggest supporter and funder of school reform, the Bill & Melinda Gates Foundation, has in the past required complete autonomy as a "nonnegotiable," as if the public schools they were supporting were charters or independent schools. Though districts may have assented to such demands in order to obtain funding, tensions inevitably arose between the proposed reforms and a district's curriculum or staffing agenda—not to mention state laws.

For her part, Ciancio insisted from the beginning that small schools in Mapleton would never operate outside of district control—a stance that did not prevent her from obtaining Gates support. Early on, she introduced the term "agency" to replace the term "autonomy," a substitution that softens the connotation of independence and conjures the image of a sub-office to a central corporation. School directors were well advised to adopt the perspective implied by the substitution.

We believe that autonomy, at least as it was conceived in the early years of small school reform, is neither possible nor desirable in the context of public schools. A school in a public school environment never stands alone, just as accountability never resides solely within a school—particularly in a standards-driven environment. As long as the public school operates within the context of the laws and policies of a district and state system, autonomy as it is popularly conceived is simply impossible. There will always be tensions between school and district leaders as they negotiate specific and global issues. Power will shift from one to the other in varying degrees, from one issue to another. Ultimately, however, control rests with the district. If compromise is impossible, the district nearly always wins.

School directors in Mapleton find that districtwide structures and policies sometimes serve, and sometimes thwart, their purposes:

> I think the biggest challenge for me has been trying to balance the kind of entrepreneurial spirit [you might find in a charter school] with the confines of still working within a traditional district, where you still have some traditional rules and roles and responsibilities. There are some times where I wish I had more freedom altogether. And there

are some times where I'm so thankful for the district infrastructure. (Lewis)

We conclude this chapter with advice from the field. Mapleton's budget director, when asked what he would want to tell other districts considering the kind of reforms Mapleton has implemented, responded, "I'd want them to know that you're going to struggle with autonomy constantly, and we still aren't anywhere near past that debate."

CHAPTER FOUR

Experiencing Small Schools

Teachers' and Students' Perspectives

In chapter 3, we tried to capture the challenges that Mapleton faced in implementing a reform designed to bring about fundamental changes in school cultures and classroom practices. Now the question arises: Did the district pull it off? School reforms are often implemented ineffectually, or on a lesser scale than their proponents intended. Sometimes they are never implemented at all. Without evidence that a reform was actually put in place—that it influenced teaching and learning in the ways that its advocates promised—one cannot reliably link it to subsequent academic outcomes.

From our own interviews, and from evaluation reports commissioned by the district, we conclude that, overall, Mapleton's small school reform was successfully implemented.[1] That is, small schools were created along the lines that the reformers envisioned. This is a remarkable achievement for a small, urban district, and it distinguishes Mapleton's efforts from most intended reforms, including many far more modest in scope.

In this chapter, we present our findings about how the Mapleton reform looked and felt to participants on the ground. Did small schools result in the improved engagement that district educators hoped for? Did instruction become less traditional and more constructivist? Were school cultures more welcoming to students? Did students and teachers develop better relationships? Did curriculum become more relevant to students? These were the questions we addressed to students and teachers, and for the most part, they answered in the affirmative. Again and again, we heard that the small schools had made a radical difference in how young people and adults experienced education in Mapleton.

Of course, the ambitions of the reform extended beyond such changes. The logic model postulated that by strengthening relationships and increasing student engagement, small schools would promote academic achievement and raise graduation rates. In chapter 5, we will present evidence concerning the reform's impact in those areas.

TEACHERS' PERSPECTIVES ON THE REFORM

The Mapleton reform provided an opportunity for teachers to be part of a coordinated effort to improve their schools, instruction, and relationships with students. The comments of two teachers reflect sentiments heard throughout our interviews:

> I knew we were going to have to do something drastic if we wanted to see drastic changes in our test scores. (Wegner)

> I came to a point in my life where I was teaching for two years and said, "This is not working." And so that frustration was enough for me to say, "Okay, I'll change whatever needs to be changed." And I think a lot of my colleagues feel the same way. They just realized that it was not working, and so that was motivation enough. (Brame)

In the discussion that follows, we will examine changes that teachers found in their work responsibilities and environment as a result of small school reform.

Adopting Constructivist Teaching Practices and Beliefs

In our interviews, Mapleton teachers identified several ways in which the reform altered their classroom practices. The most notable change they discussed was a shift from direct instruction to project management, from performing the role of a traditional teacher to serving as more of a facilitator or coach. The small school models required teachers to develop new ways of presenting information, alter their assessment and classroom-management practices, and create meaningful learning experiences tailored to individual students, using projects that were aligned with each school's distinctive approach and the students' needs:

> My old way of teaching was, I would have a geography textbook and we would cover a couple of chapters, have a quiz, and go on to a couple of more chapters. Now I don't use a text anymore . . . I'm teaching geography much differently than I did this time last year. I'm covering less but I am covering it deeper. (Brame)

> I think I am seeing more and more that my teaching needs to be for all of my students, not just a homogeneous mass in the middle. I need to direct my teaching by differentiating to address all the different needs of the students in my room. And that's something I never really tried to do before. (Steiner)

Admittedly, some teachers have struggled to make the transition:

> It has been difficult for me. There are these areas that I want the kids to work on . . . and I really want to be able to tie this to the school's [constructivist] approach. Sometimes I can, and sometimes I can't. I think, "There's got to be a creative, unique way to get to that match." So then I am just kind of wrestling with, "Well, maybe I should go back to my own ways." (Wegner)

One teacher recalled that when he moved from direct instruction to a project-based approach, he began talking less and the students talked more. At first, this made him uncomfortable. He said, "With direct instruction, I would be in control. You know, every minute you want to be the one saying, "Okay, now here's where we are, now take out your paper, now do this, now put this away." However, once he realized that "giving up control" created opportunities for the students to take responsibility for their own learning, he became more at ease with the process.

In February 2006 and March 2007, Dr. Kevin Welner, an independent evaluator and professor at the University of Colorado, Boulder, submitted evaluation reports that echoed what we heard in our interviews:[2] "Generally speaking, teachers in the new small schools were enthusiastic about how the reform has changed instruction. One aspect of this change mentioned by several teachers was the movement toward depth over breadth. Another is the shifting of responsibility for learning from the teacher to the student."[3]

Welner recounted a conversation with one teacher who was struggling to keep his students on track during project-based lessons. Welner asked whether a more traditional instructional approach might reduce the number of "students doing things that aren't related to the class." The teacher replied that, in the long run, the answer was no. He wanted his classroom to be a place where students "had opportunities to talk about things," and he was convinced that, over time, the students would learn when it was appropriate to socialize and when they needed to focus on their work. If he gave up and went back to his old methods, the teacher said, the students would be bored and disengaged.[4]

Teachers Influence Schools

Involvement in the Mapleton reform was a positive and empowering process for many district teachers. Although they described the process as extremely demanding of their time and talents, it was clear that they welcomed the opportunity to help design and implement the changes necessary to create small schools:

> Part of the [school] model is, teachers get to say things about what's happening and propose things . . . I think that's the piece of it that's kept us alive so far. As long as that piece is still there, there is hope. (Benio)

There were about seven of us who were selected to be in the [school] design team, and it was tremendously empowering. I think it was the excitement of being involved in something that's really new, and I think that really kept us going. (Brame)

Although the challenges associated with implementing and sustaining these changes were enormous, Welner found that school directors and teachers generally had no desire to return to "a more traditional way." He noted their commitment to reforming both classroom practices and the larger school culture:

Educators at each of the six small schools have made a conscious and concentrated effort to create a healthy school culture. For most, this is the key, necessary precondition to making their school function as designed and desired. As one teacher explained, "You can't skirt the issue [of school culture] . . . and hope to see academic progress. Because in my short-lived experience, it won't happen. It simply won't happen."[5]

Teachers felt an increased sense of shared responsibility for meeting their schools' learning goals:

Changes? First off, I collaborate . . . My teaching is not my own. It's now part of a ninth-grade team and part of the school's team. So I've opened up my door and my lesson plans and my thinking to my colleagues. And that's exciting. Something about the old teaching I hated was [that] we never knew what anybody else was doing. I felt like I was on my own, and we really didn't share help or support or anything like that . . . I never really had any feedback on whether I was being effective or not. But now I get that feedback all the time. And I have opportunities to share what I am doing and struggling with. (Brame)

Whereas faculty meetings prior to the reform were often gripe sessions, now they are described as more participatory, professional, and productive. Teachers have more time to problem solve together, and they make decisions about all aspects of schooling. In some schools, teachers meet daily and therefore feel that they are on the "same page." In addition, there seems to be an increased sense among the teachers that they are being treated with respect by colleagues and administrators:

> It used to be, "Here are the new things that you have to do. Please fill out this form and show that you are doing it." And now . . . we argue about things and we come up with new ideas and propose things and find better ways to do them. (Benio)

> I don't have to worry about my boss doing something behind my back to me . . . We don't act childish with each other—you know, talking about this person over here and this person over here. We are so small, we just can't—we couldn't survive if that was what was happening. (Krane)

Welner reported in 2006 that a culture of collaboration was emerging in the small schools. He also cited the comments of another professor and evaluator of the reform, Dr. Patrick McQuillan, who noted:

> In speaking with and observing some teachers, I saw how they often have substantive conversations with their colleagues or persons from outside the schools, such as representatives of Expeditionary Learning. Even our group interview with the principals/directors included a measure of substantive conversation, as the participants did not merely respond directly to each of our questions, but they often modified, clarified, or added to things their colleagues said.[6]

In the following year, Welner reported more variation in teachers' attitudes. Still, comments about school culture were predominantly positive:

> School communities for staff appear to be quickly and reliably taking hold. The following comment is representative: "I think the work environment's great. I love working here. I think [the director

is] probably the best administrator I've ever worked for, and . . . I've been teaching quite a few years. He's supportive of teachers. He'll listen to you . . . " Teachers often mentioned their colleagues' support, too. They told us about how they felt comfortable asking for advice and sharing ideas. Simply put, they like their workplaces more, and this improvement seems to be due to the small learning communities that have been formed.[7]

Meaningful Professional Development

During each school's first year, the district conducted most professional development activities, while the model partners and affiliated organizations provided others. Teachers spoke highly of the opportunities that the model partners offered: "The New Tech model does an unbelievably great job of preparing a teacher . . . Any training you want, and are willing to do, you can learn it. I mean, they will teach it to you. They pay for it; they fly us out and put us up." (Fulbright)

Teachers also spoke appreciatively about opportunities to connect to a professional community of educators outside of the district. Most agreed that the workshops and conferences were effective at teaching and inspiring them to adopt the essentials of each small school model in their classrooms:

> The main reason I go is because the people involved in this movement are just the smartest, most amazing people that I interact with. So I would never give up that opportunity. I mean, it's just this amazing, amazing experience to go and meet with all of these minds and talk about what's going on at all these different schools and see what's really working at another school so maybe you can bring that back to your school and try it here. (Krane)

These are the venues, teachers said, where they learned what it means to create an integrated curriculum, facilitate small-group work, become reflective practitioners, differentiate instruction, or create inquiry-based classrooms.

Back in their schools, many teachers worked with instructional coaches provided either by the district or by the model partners. In addition, as Welner reported in 2007, the teachers coached one another:

> Feedback from teachers about the district's professional development has been overwhelmingly positive. Some spoke of how they and their colleagues shaped their own approaches and often relied on internal expertise. This allows them to reinforce each other's learning. For instance, the teachers at [Welby New Tech] use "critical friends" protocols, presenting their curriculum to each other.[8]

Better Relationships with Students and Parents

Many teachers find that their interactions with students have changed for the better in the small schools. They say that they know their students as learners and as people on a much deeper level and that they are able to maintain these relationships over a longer period of time. "It used to be that you could be a student nobody knew very well. You could be a student that was just a name, and we didn't even know what happened—you could drop out or transfer away . . . But that no longer happens now. Now I know all my students, even the ones that only come once or twice." (Benio)

Many teachers also say that they have a more personal relationship with their students' parents and families. This is a result of the structural changes required by the small school models. In some schools, teachers have the opportunity to remain with the same cohort of students for grades 9–12. They are required to obtain parent input while developing student learning plans. Teachers say that the resulting relationships create a more satisfying work environment and enable them to provide students with individualized support:

> It's easier for me to focus and to really think, "Okay, I can sit down and just think about Jaclyn's test scores." And I can do it for a whole hour. You know—look at her stuff, go through it. Say, "Oh, this is what she needs." And then I can be creative about how to incorporate or help her incorporate [the learning] into her project. (Steiner)

Every week I sit down [with each student] for at least fifteen minutes. We always talk about planning: "So what are you working on? What are you doing? What did you finish? Are you going to get enough done for the trimester? Do you need to step it up? Are you going too fast?" We also look at things like test scores . . . what areas are improving and what areas are not. (White)

Mapleton's small schools also use innovative organizational structures to give students a voice and promote engagement: "We have these things called town meetings, and more and more kids are starting to be participating in them . . . Last time, they were framed around, 'How can we ensure a school culture of respect and learning?' And every kid can go up and really voice what they think is happening or should happen." (Sorenson)

These changes have clearly improved the overall school climate for this group of teachers. They are more invested in the process of teaching, feel empowered to make positive changes in their workplace, and believe student performance will improve as a result.

Challenges for Teachers

While the teachers we interviewed agreed on the benefits of the reform, they also acknowledged that the transition to small schools had not been easy. They had been required to alter nearly every aspect of their professional practice and to embrace approaches that were new to many of them: "The most challenging thing for me was being twenty to twenty-five years into my career and then saying, 'I'm willing to change and do things totally different from what I've done for all that time.' It's like you're committing to a whole new concept of teaching." (Fulbright)

For teachers trained in traditional methods, learning a new set of instructional strategies would have been daunting enough. But the challenge was exacerbated by the rapid pace of the reform. Mapleton's teachers had to learn *and* implement the new strategies simultaneously: "It's like we're changing a tire on a bus that's going forty miles an hour. I think in retrospect, if this were a process we could have done in ten years instead of two, that would have been better." (Brame)

As we have seen, teachers generally appreciated the professional development offered by the district and the model partners. But several said that they didn't have time to take full advantage of these opportunities—and some don't have time even now. To understand why, we have to consider not only the pace of the reform, but also its scope.

Even as teachers tried to adopt new instructional techniques, they were also expected to write curriculum; manage increased parent contact; participate in student advising, counseling, and discipline; assume an active role in school governance; and engage in intensive professional development. While each of these areas created challenges for teachers, the greatest challenge was being responsible for all of them at once.

In the new small schools, teachers found themselves carrying out duties formerly associated with other staff positions: "We are not just teachers—we're counselors and administrators . . . Sometimes, the added responsibilities have been really hard." (Brame) With fewer full-time employees in each building (including reduced support staff), faculty members who used to teach one subject are now responsible for teaching several. And since small schools in Mapleton lack assistant principals, discipline must be managed largely in the classroom.

In his Year One evaluation, Welner expressed concerns about this aspect of the reform. "The district administration," he wrote, "has been up-front about the fact that they are placing great demands and high expectations on their teachers. But such honesty does not preclude burnout, stress, and simple inability to do all necessary work."[9] Some of the teachers Welner interviewed that first year sounded overwhelmed: "I just feel like I'm so swamped. I'd like to survive right now." Others embraced their expanded roles but didn't gloss over the costs:

> I work really, really long hours. It's very common for me to be here until 8, 9 o'clock at night. But that's my choice . . . Things that I'm doing are writing lessons or coming up with lessons . . . Structuring what I want students to be talking about or discussing. Grading papers. Coming up with better systems for myself in how I organize myself . . . Calling parents. I'm in constant communication with parents.[10]

Welner argued that the sustainability of the reform depended, in part, on reducing the demands placed on teachers. He also recognized that teachers would remain committed to the goals of the reform only if they had some success in achieving them. Thus, he advised the district to enhance professional development in one critical area—differentiating instruction to meet each student's needs:

Mapleton's overall record of providing professional development and other supports is commendable. However, it is becoming clear that a considerable subset of teachers and students need more . . . [T]each- ers who feel little success at differentiating instruction for a heteroge- neous class will no longer buy into this key, high-expectations aspect of Mapleton's reform.[11]

In addition, teachers told us that they wanted to learn how they could get students to "develop good questions, deeper-level questions," so that their projects would not be superficial. And some teachers felt that increased contact with parents required new communication skills. "I think that's probably an area of growth that a lot of us are still work- ing on," one teacher said.

Changing Parents' and Students' Expectations About School

Parents' and students' preexisting expectations about instructional meth- ods, content, and discipline—their images of what school "is supposed to be"—created challenges for teachers. Many parents had qualms about the break from what they considered to be essential elements of school- ing. Teachers had to learn quickly how to address their concerns:

[That] first year, it was very hard for a lot of parents because they were like, "So what are they doing in algebra class?" "Well, we don't have algebra class." And they would ask, "What do you mean you don't have algebra class? How are they going to get into college?" So I would explain, "Well, we are a research-based model, and the school that it is based on has graduated eight classes, and in those classes 90 percent have entered some sort of postsecondary education." (Krane)

Teachers told us that changing parents' ideas about schools will take time and will only happen as parents see and experience the results. One recalled a father who came to school to hear his son's presentation:

> He says, "Well, I don't really like these presentations. When I was in high school, we had final tests, and I just think that prepares students better." . . . Afterwards, he came up to me and said, "You know what? This prepares my kid much better for the real world than any test ever would, because I can see him thinking and presenting and putting a lot of things together." (Brame)

Many teachers want to see the district make a more concerted effort to help parents understand the benefits and limitations of small schools. For example, small schools in Mapleton, as elsewhere across the country, do not offer a full menu of electives such as art, music, and drama, nor do they necessarily have smaller class sizes than traditional schools do.

Teachers also believe that parents need more information about how to choose a school best suited to their child and should be made aware of the importance of being involved in this decision: "A lot of students picked schools based on their friends, where their friends were going. So, not the ideal situation . . . I don't think that kids will make decisions based on what schools meet their learning styles unless parents are involved." (Brame)

While students were attracted to the promise of small schools, most had never experienced anything other than an impersonal, rule-driven, traditional school culture. All at once, they had to revise their understanding of what school is and what their roles and responsibilities should be:

> Most of [the students] want to be told, "Take your book out, open your book to this page, close your book, now let's go over here, now let's go." They want to be told that. That's how they've been educated for however many years. And it's hard for them to realize, "Hey, I am responsible for deadlines. I am responsible for someone else as well as for myself." (Fulbright)

The small school models emphasize shared governance and opportunities for students to create standards and norms of behavior. Students are also responsible for dealing with the consequences when the norms are broken. This can be difficult for students who have just spent ten years in schools where teachers or principals dole out punishments: "We are really strong on student voice and student governance and democracy and letting them have a voice in their learning and their school. And the biggest shock to me is that they don't want it. They don't want responsibility for themselves. And that's something that we are working on." (Brame)

Comments from teachers provided both evidence of struggle and signs of hope:

> The students complain that we're asking them to do work. We're holding the kids' feet to the fire much more, trying to follow the [school] model, which is college prep. And so our culture this year is in flux . . . [The students are] pushing back a lot . . . They don't like the fact that they can't hide in the back of the room and not do any work and overwhelm the teacher with the 115 kids that he sees a day. [The kids are also] rebelling because [teachers are] calling home so much. (Kennedy)

> [A]t the beginning of the year, we had about 40 percent of the kids turning [their work] in on time. Now that they've been doing this for a while, we're in the fourteenth week of the year, the last big project we had in math, over 90 percent turned it in on the day it was due . . . They're seeing it as more real, more practical, something that's more worthwhile to them. (Thompson)

STUDENTS' PERSPECTIVES ON THE REFORM

This section highlights the perspectives of those the Mapleton reform is intended to serve—the students. We asked students currently attending a variety of Mapleton high schools what it was like to live through the district's transition and what their individual experiences have been in their new schools.

School Choice: Not Students' First Choice

When the district first announced the decision to reinvent the comprehensive high school by creating several small schools, many students reacted negatively. Although the students understood the reasons for the reform—poor performance on CSAP, increasing dropout rates, declining enrollment—they were concerned about missing out on what they referred to as the "best parts" of high school:

> I've always wanted to go to Skyview, like my big brothers. Both of them have been there. I went to school with my older brother once and saw my brother at school one time and saw the halls filled and him smiling and walking down the hall and everybody knowing him. And I kind of miss that . . . I kind of wanted to go to a big school and feel the bigness of it. (James)

Some were looking forward to attending the same high school where older siblings or other relatives had graduated; others were excited about football games, proms, and yearbooks; and some were looking forward to the promise of "high school drama," which includes dating, gossip, fights, and the challenge of finding their niche. Students thought that once Skyview was broken apart, they would miss their chance to be part of *Friday Night Lights*, Mapleton style.

Many students also experienced frustration and anxiety about having to leave friends and close relationships behind as they transitioned to their new schools:

> When it first broke up, I didn't want to lose my friends, I didn't want to have to move [to a different school], I didn't want to have to catch a school bus. It was more like, "I just got here and now we're breaking up again . . . I have to meet new friends again, I've got to do everything all over again and I just got the feel of high school. (Rachel)

Students from the class of 2006 remained at Skyview during its last year of operation as a comprehensive high school, but they shared the campus with two small schools that enrolled freshmen and sophomores. Meanwhile, the district was busy opening additional small high schools

elsewhere in the district. As a result, energy was diverted from Skyview, throwing traditional activities—prom, yearbook, and even sports
events—into the background. Many from the class of 2006 felt cheated
of their senior year. While Mapleton administrators and teachers did what
they could to provide these students with a rich experience, the effort to
create the infrastructure for four new high schools inevitably drew attention away from the class participating in the traditional model.

Seniors in the class of 2007 experienced these feelings even more
acutely. One student referred to this class as "the lost cohort." Seniors
in the previous year could at least ride out their experience at Skyview.
But when students in the class of 2007 entered their last year of high
school, they had to pick new schools to attend. One senior described
her response when she learned about the reinvention: "I felt lost . . . and
a lot of students left because they felt lost. They went to different districts . . . I have friends that totally dropped out because they didn't
know what to do." (Ana)

As the reinvention began, freshmen, sophomores, and juniors were
faced with the challenge of choosing a new school. Many students found
that, in fact, they had no choice—they were forced to attend the school
selected for them by a parent or guardian. Other students became active
participants in the decision-making process. Students involved in choosing their new school were asked to define their individual learning style,
identify personal interests, and specify their educational needs. Still, the
menu of school options was baffling, and students felt that they lacked
a clear vision of the day-to-day reality of each school. This confusion
was exacerbated by pressure to make their decisions quickly.

As a result, many students made decisions based on noninstructional
factors, such as social reasons or convenience. For example, many students chose the school that their friends had decided to attend. Student
athletes chose MESA or Skyview Academy (housed in the building of
the original Skyview High School) because sports practices would take
place on the campus.

Eventually, students learned from their mistakes or the mistakes of
others. They had lots of advice for future students on how to choose a
school:

I guess the best advice is, don't go to what school your friends are going to, because that is not going to help you. Just because your friends are going there, whoop-ti-doo. These schools are made specifically so that you can learn the way you need to learn—the way that's best for you. (Mateo)

I would tell them, "Go to the school itself and talk to the head person or the principal. Talk to your friends, and talk to Mapleton school district and ask them what it is like. Ask, 'What are the guidelines at this school?' Look at what this school will really teach you, and look at its focus." (Jesus)

One student had this suggestion for school administrators, to help students make informed decisions: "Instead of telling them [students] what's best about your school, tell everything. Tell the pros and cons . . . You should have a little conversation about what's bad about the school. You should show everything, not just the good side." (James) Although students acknowledged the district's efforts to communicate essential information about the new schools, they still feel that they would have made better choices if they had known more about each school.

New Schools, New Rules

Once at their new schools, students experienced myriad challenges. Unfamiliar teachers, buildings, schedules, curricula, and peers created anxiety and stress. One of the most difficult adjustments was learning to meet a brand-new set of expectations: "[During the transition] there would be times I'd be like, 'Forget this school. I am going back to traditional.' I couldn't deal with all the work. I couldn't deal with me having to be the teacher or in taking that step to be like, 'I want to do this.' I was so much more used to people handing me stuff and saying, 'Go ahead, do that.'" (Rachel)

Students quickly learned that in order to succeed at their new schools, they would have to adopt a new way of thinking about their education. This meant playing an active role in their own learning and taking on increased responsibilities, including designing learning plans and projects, assessing their own work, and helping to create the school culture. When asked to compare teachers' expectations of them in their new schools and in their previous schools, students said:

> We're expected to do better. We take it upon ourselves as students to catch each other when we are not doing things right. Usually, people just keep quiet in traditional school if somebody is disrupting their learning environment. But we actually take charge of that—"Like, can you please be quiet?"—and things like that. (Brittney)

> Yeah, there's a lot more weight on our shoulders, but it's like a good responsibility and a good weight . . . because it prepares you for the weight that's going to be in college and in real life. It's not about math anymore. It's about my life and responsibility. (James)

> One thing that people need to know is that they need to be ready to be challenged. Get ready to be challenged. (Jesus)

Students are both appreciative and resentful of their new role in designing and implementing the school culture. While they enjoy having "voice" or input into decisions concerning school policies about discipline issues and important elements of school life, they also experience this as a burden. Many students acknowledged a need for adult guidance as they gradually became accustomed to their new role in school governance. This was especially important when dealing with discipline policies and practices: "There are still people who mess around, and teachers don't do anything to them . . . . It's usually the students that have to get involved . . . There's no actual reward for people that do good, but no actual discipline for people doing bad. So we are kind of stuck in the middle. I think it's chaos sometimes." (Michael) In some schools, students said the lack of discipline often resulted in conflicts between students and became a serious obstacle to learning.

In general, students find the course work at their new schools more demanding and time-consuming than ever before. Most of the students we interviewed described an increased emphasis on "real-world learning," which they defined in terms of changes in the physical environment of the school, differences in the way they are treated by teachers, and a sense that schoolwork has become relevant to their lives.

Those who mentioned changes in the physical environment said that their new schools motivate them and create conditions in which they can do their best work. Students expressed an appreciation for clean halls, comfortable desks and chairs, natural light, and the freedom to move around the building and school grounds.

> It's like, walking through the hallways, there's windows in the classrooms. You can watch everyone work, and it's just open. It's a more comfortable environment, instead of being in what a lot of kids refer to as "my penitentiary." . . . So it is different here. The feel is more comfortable. It's not dreading going to school or feeling like you are locked up. (Julia)

Not all students experienced this positive change. At the beginning of the first year of implementation (2004–05), there was some confusion about students' placements and district policies related to new schools. Some students did not have a school to call home. Instead, they were shuffled from building to building as the district tried to decide where to house all the new schools. This left many students feeling unsettled. There were also complaints about restrictions on student mobility within school campuses. Could a student attending MESA, for example, visit a friend attending Skyview, which was housed in the same facility? Such issues were compounded by the fact that each school now had its own rules and policies, which many students interpreted as arbitrary and unfair.

Improved Student-Teacher Relationships

Whatever their ambivalence about other features of their small schools, students we interviewed were unanimous in celebrating a dramatic shift in their relationships with teachers. When asked, "What's the best thing about being at this school for you?" many remarked that they felt more respected, trusted, and known, often referring to quality "one-on-one time" with teachers:

Here you get the individual attention you need from your teacher and you build that relationship with the teachers, instead of you're just a grade and that's it. You're actually a person and they get to know your family. (Janelle)

I think it's the student relationships with their teachers. I don't have to be scheduled in for a time to talk to them; I can talk to them in class and everything. They also know what is going on in my personal life. (Brittney)

The way the teachers treat you is professional. You know, they'll remind you that you need to get your work done, but they won't be like, "Come on, Mateo, come on, Mateo." They'll be like, "You need to get it done, and if you don't, you know it's on you. It's your responsibility." (Mateo)

Even though class sizes didn't decrease as a result of the reform, students said that teachers in their small schools knew them better than the teachers in their previous schools did:

The teachers are able to know your strengths and weaknesses. My English teacher knows I am a strong writer, but my communications need some help. My math teacher knows what kind of style wording he needs to teach me things. History, she knows how I write and what kind of student I am, and if I am going to speak out in a discussion or if she needs to find another way to get me to show my views of what we read. (Brittney)

We have an advisory class almost every day . . . We have our chance to sit in there and go through our grades: "This is what I am missing in this class." We have afterschool study or support three days a week. You can stay until 5:00, and different teachers sponsor that and you can get stuff done. But it's stuff like that you can take advantage of and step up and be responsible for your own education. (Julia)

In small schools, teachers stay informed about attendance, missed work, and students' struggles. Students spoke appreciatively about being recognized for their strengths and supported in areas where they needed to improve. They enjoy the personal attention and especially the feeling that someone at school is looking out for them. "At normal schools you can slink off into the corner and become that recluse. But here, you can't. Like, if you are not here, someone is going to—I've had calls from teachers: 'Hey, are you OK? Where you at?'" (Julia)

Attending a school in which teachers have the organizational support to engage with their students has created an "atmosphere of care." For some students, the contrast with their earlier school experiences could not be more pronounced:

> At my old school I had one teacher who would tell me every single day that I wouldn't make it, that I was going to fail, that I never would make it to college, that I was going to be a drugged-up, dropout, teen mom. That's not what a kid needs to hear going through school. I mean, here it's encouraging and supportive. They treat you like you are human, and they're human, too, you know . . . I am from the failure students who hated school. [Now] I don't want to leave. (Julia)

Re-learning Learning

Along with increased responsibilities, higher expectations for student performance, and improved student-teacher relationships, students spoke eloquently about differences in instructional practices. They attributed most of the changes primarily to "the way we are learning" and not necessarily to changes in content. The following excerpt illustrates a common experience among those students who talked with us:

INTERVIEWER: Do you see big changes between how you learn in school now as compared to how you learned then?

JAMES: Yeah. I always use the math example, because in eighth grade you would learn long division, and you would get a big sheet of paper, a packet maybe, just fill them out, and that would be your learning.

INTERVIEWER: OK.

JAMES: Like the teacher would show you how to learn, show you it, and then you would repeat problems. Like here, we'd have one long-division problem, and that one problem can teach me more than that packet, because it is more intuitive thinking and more critical thinking.

INTERVIEWER: Do you feel challenged here as a student?

JAMES: Yeah, I am constantly thinking. We were talking about it in class today, and we could be asked one question a day and we would probably learn and discuss more than most schools would do in a whole day . . . [I]nstead of getting asked fifteen mindless questions, you get one open-ended question like, "Why would that be?" And you're like, you have to think about a few of those things. And there's always someone disagreeing with that. And you always change your views and just learn new things because that one question is like, is powerful.

Another student described the difference in this way:

I have learned more here. I always did good in school, but I didn't necessarily get what I was doing. But here, you have to know what you are learning, because you have to present it in front of a panel at the end of every trimester. They have the power to say, "I don't think this student should pass." So you really want to prove to your panelist that you know what you are talking about. So therefore you go much more into depth with your projects. (Gabrielle)

Students approve of most of the instructional changes because they believe they are learning more and because the material seems applicable to life outside of school. "You learn a lot more hands-on. It isn't just sitting in the classroom and doing textbook work. It's actually going out into the community and understanding where you live, what life is all about." (Jerilyn)

Most students agreed that their new schools afford them a variety of interesting and motivating opportunities for learning. For many, this is accomplished through projects that allow them to explore personal interests.

> I like the projects . . . The work is connected to real-life experiences. Like, I love football, and last year in Algebra we had to do a project with the football players. We had to see how fast they run and their agility and all that. I actually wanted to do the work. It wasn't like you had to do it. It was because I wanted to do it. (Mary Ellen)

> What we learn here is what we want to learn, so it is a big difference. It's not like, "You have to learn this about science to pass." We are learning what we want to learn about, but we are still getting our math, science, our language arts, communication, everything. (Janelle)

Students also enjoy the opportunity to develop skills not emphasized in their previous schools, such as public speaking, teamwork, and time management. Several students explained how project-based learning has helped increase their level of self-confidence:

> My grades were really bad, and I always felt really stupid. But I guess I'm pretty smart, according to everyone else. But I mean, it's just coming here and doing these projects and actually being involved in my work. It makes me feel better, because I realize, you know, I can do this stuff. I'm not stupid. (Mateo)

> I feel like I am more of a student here and more appreciated at this school . . . I feel better about myself. I feel that I am a student learning on my own and through help. So I'm learning more, actually. I feel good about that. (Kevin)

Small-group projects require students to divide labor and depend on one another. Although many students value this as an opportunity to learn how to collaborate with others, some find it difficult to work with classmates with varied abilities and levels of motivation, especially when the whole group is held accountable for the final product. As one student explained: "For example, if I am getting straight As and that person, he isn't doing well in school, he'll tend to not do his work. So it's hard, you know, it's hard to keep up with that—keep up with your work and also have to keep up with the work he isn't doing." (Jesus)

Students also struggle with the grading structures in the Mapleton high schools. They say it is more difficult to achieve high grades because schools have changed the criteria. For example, in order to receive an A, students must demonstrate learning at a "deeper level." While many understand the concept of depth, some students are confused about how to demonstrate their mastery of the material.

Some schools are no longer using letter grades. For students who are accustomed to receiving grades as a reward for their work, doing without them can be a challenge. "We don't get grades, and we usually have to do presentations about what we have learned. A lot of times, I find it hard to motivate myself to do it." (Jenna)

Improved Social Climate

The Mapleton reform has resulted in what many students describe as a radical change in school climate. Many students we interviewed were surprised to find a richer and more satisfying social scene in their new schools. Small schools have encouraged young people to challenge their preconceptions about members of their school community. They create opportunities to forge friendships and emotional ties with people they used to think of as different from themselves. "I never thought who my best friend is now would ever be my friend. She's like this Goth, punk-rocker type of person. And here's me: I'm like the preppy little girl and goody two-shoes. She used to smoke stuff, and I never thought in a million years I'd be her best friend." (Gabrielle)

During interviews, students were passionate about the changes in their school community:

I guess we just know each other . . . We can use each other, and we can trust each other in our learning. We can always go to each other and know they're going to be there for us . . . We're like a very big family, I guess is how you could describe us. (Jerilyn)

When I walk through the doors, I have people that care about me unconditionally. Whether I have an A in the class or an F, whether I had gotten in trouble yesterday or not gotten in trouble for a year, I'm cared about. It's just unconditional. That's probably the best thing. It's a community that I have. Students, staff, and everyone here—well, almost everybody here—cares about me and wants to see me succeed in life. And they will all do their best to have me do that. (James)

Students report a dramatic decrease in exclusionary social behavior and conflicts among students. Many believe that the new environment has created social opportunities they did not have in their previous schools. "Shoot, you go to another school—you know, a regular high school—you have people you don't like, you have your crew, you have your preps, jocks, [Goths], and little thugs. You've got 'em all. Then you come to a school like this and you are all one." (Kevin)

Students who used to feel threatened or mistreated at school now feel safe and accepted. "I was teased a lot in my middle school and was bullied, so I didn't want to go to school. But now, it's like, 'Oh, I really like school.' I have friends [who] are not going to judge me because I do well in school." (Gabrielle)

When students spoke of the changes in school climate and their strong connections to their school communities, some confessed that they miss the drama they were expecting in their high school years, and some said the social scene at their school was boring. But other students indicated that the transition had brought about a shift in their priorities: "I realized that we are at school for a reason, and that's to learn and to graduate and go on to college. And that's my main focus right now." (Mary Ellen)

According to the students, the cohesiveness of the small schools is accompanied by one disadvantage: the sense that students in one school are isolated from their peers elsewhere in the district. This is mostly due to what the students described as "poor communication" between schools as well as between central administration and the multiple school sites. Students want more information about what is happening in the greater Mapleton community, and specifically about dances, basketball games, and other important events in the lives of youth. Several students suggested that the district create a Web site where they could post details about upcoming events.

Like the teachers, students had mixed reactions to the changes brought about by small school reform. Most students we interviewed were positive about the changes. But no student reported that school was the same in the small school environment as it had been in the traditional schools they had previously attended. According to those teachers and students we interviewed, education in Mapleton had changed in many of the ways that the district's leaders had hoped it would.

CHAPTER FIVE

Is the Reform Working?

In chapters 3 and 4, we addressed one of the key questions raised by any reform: Was it actually implemented? As we have seen, Mapleton defied the odds by creating several small high schools, nearly all of them based on national models. And to judge from the testimony of teachers and students in the district, classrooms in these new schools functioned very differently from those in traditional schools. Thus, if we were asked whether anything really changed in Mapleton as a result of the reform, our answer would be yes.

In this chapter, we address two further questions:

1. How did the district respond to early CSAP scores indicating that the reform had limited impact on student achievement?

2. If school climate improved and student engagement rose, why didn't CSAP scores increase in Mapleton?

Before we present the data from the early years of the reform, it is worth recalling the mind-set of directors and their staffs as they were creating the new small schools. At that time, the directors were preoccupied with implementing the models that district leaders had brought to Mapleton:

We made a very conscious effort to focus on being a good replication of the model last year. And that, in and of itself, is a ton of work. And so, sometimes, comments would come back to me saying, "Person X in the central administration office is concerned that there's not much literacy instruction going on over there." Or, "We're very worried that your teachers don't have the ELL strategies that they need." But I said, "We're focusing on [implementing the model]. And yes, these things are important, but I will burn out every single teacher within three months if I try to get all those initiatives done." (Simons)

It isn't as if the directors were indifferent to literacy instruction or ELL (English language learner) strategies. But they trusted the logic of the reform: if they faithfully replicated the models, then test scores would inevitably rise:

The way I say it to my staff is that if we do things the way that we're supposed to do, then our kids will improve their performance. Because what we're doing is an investment in each of the students, their potential and their abilities, and because of that, we're going to have an impact on kids . . . [T]hey'll show up better on those tests because they're more invested. (Resnick)

District administrators supported this focus, and so did the state's accreditation officer, even though he wasn't initially convinced by Mapleton's approach: "I also went out and visited every [Mapleton] school this fall . . . There's an ownership developing around those individual schools that you would anticipate kids would like, and the teachers chose to be here, and the principal wants to run this kind of school. And you know, I think that can be translated into performance in terms of achievement." (Phillips)

CSAP RESULTS

Unfortunately, CSAP results released in summer 2006 did not indicate the swift academic turnaround that many in Mapleton had hoped for. Although 5 percent more tenth-graders tested proficient or better in reading compared to the previous year, math proficiency dropped by 2 percent, and the students' performance on all tests was well below that of Colorado students generally. A year later, in 2007, tenth-grade reading proficiency was up again, this time by eight percentage points. But writing proficiency dropped by two percentage points and math showed another 2 percent decline. The 2008 scores showed declines in reading and writing proficiency, while math proficiency stayed flat (table 5.1).

Scores of Mapleton's tenth-graders are graphed in figure 5.1.

District faculty, staff, and students were discouraged by these results. The dramatic gains Mapleton educators anticipated had not materialized. Still, the district found signs of improvement among students in grades 7–10. Its analyses of CSAP data are more fine-grained and nuanced than the single snapshot presented above. The following summary is excerpted from a memo presented to the school board after the July 2007 release of CSAP scores:

TABLE 5.1 Tenth grade CSAP results, 2003–08

Percentage proficient and above*

	2002–03	2003–04**	2004–05	2005–06	2006–07	2007–08
READING						
All Colorado	67	65	66	68	69	66
Mapleton	46	45	33	38	46	35
WRITING						
All Colorado	52	50	50	50	51	47
Mapleton	29	22	17	21	19	17
MATH						
All Colorado	42	27	30	31	30	30
Mapleton	8	11	9	7	5	5

Data from Colorado Department of Education: www.cde.state.co.us.
*Proficient means grade-level performance or better.
**Reform begins.

FIGURE **5.1**   Tenth graders' CSAP scores, 2003–2008

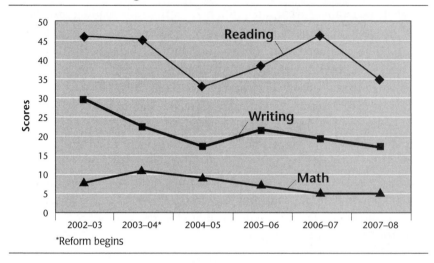

Mapleton's overall CSAP proficiency rates remain low, and actually got a little worse in 2007 compared to 2006. However, the 2007 CSAP data contain evidence of initial progress as well:

- The percentage of district CSAP test scores that moved closer to state averages increased this year compared to last year

- The gap between district and state performance averaged across all grade levels decreased in reading

- Proficiency rates increased on over half the tests administered to students in grades 7–10

- The percentage of grade-level test scores reflecting one year's growth in one year's time increased in 2007, exclusively as a result of the performance of students in grades 7–10

- Eleventh-graders' total ACT averages increased performance across the board

Taken together, the 2007 CSAP data suggest that performance declines seen in 2005 and 2006 moderated somewhat in 2007. Especially encouraging is the fact that almost all evidence of improvement is seen at grades 7–11, which are grades where the district's reinvention efforts are most mature. With the largest part of the necessary logistical restructuring activity associated with the district's reinvention plan completed, it is anticipated that these initial small successes will expand as the new schools turn their attention to maximizing the potential of their unique instructional models.[1]

As part of our research for this book, we analyzed CSAP results by ethnicity, looking at scores for Latino and Anglo (white) tenth-graders from 2003 to 2008 (these two groups make up over 90 percent of Mapleton students). In every subject area, we found significant achievement gaps between Latino and Anglo youth, but it is difficult to generalize about trends.[2] In reading, for example, the percentage of Anglo students scoring at the proficient level dropped from 57 percent to 42 percent between 2003 and 2008. In contrast, the percentage of Latino students demonstrating reading proficiency dropped from 34 percent in 2003 to 20 percent in 2005 but rose in 2006 and 2007, and rose very slightly again in 2008, to 30 percent. As a result, the achievement gap (as measured by the percentage of students scoring proficient on CSAP) narrowed from 23 percentage points in 2003 to 12 percentage points in 2008—but only because Anglo students' proficiency rates dropped far more than Latino students' rose (figure 5.2).

In writing, tenth-grade proficiency rates dropped for both groups between 2003 and 2008. The percentage of Anglo students scoring at the proficient or advanced level fell from 38.6 percent to 23.9 percent, while the percentage of Latino students scoring proficient fell from 19.6 percent to 13.4 percent. Up until 2007, it appeared that the achievement gap was widening, but it narrowed sharply in 2008, again, as in reading, due to a precipitous drop in Anglo students' scores (figure 5.3).

As noted earlier, Mapleton students' math scores have been a persistent cause of concern. The rates of proficiency among Anglo tenth graders have steadily declined since 2004. Latino students' proficiency rates have declined as well, although they did improve in 2008. Nevertheless, less than 7 percent of Anglos and 4 percent of Latinos score in the proficient range in math (figure 5.4).

FIGURE **5.2** **CSAP reading: tenth grade, 2003–08**
Percent proficient and advanced

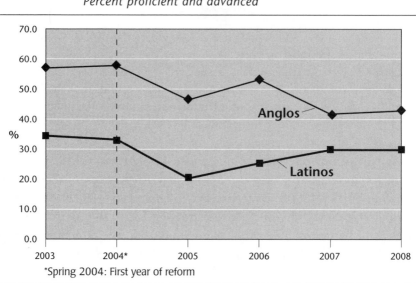

*Spring 2004: First year of reform

FIGURE **5.3** **CSAP writing: tenth grade, 2003–08**
Percent proficient and advanced

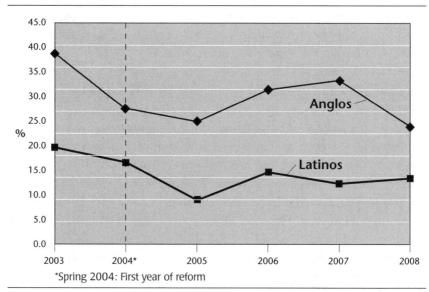

*Spring 2004: First year of reform

FIGURE 5.4   CSAP math: tenth grade, 2003–08
Percent proficient and advanced

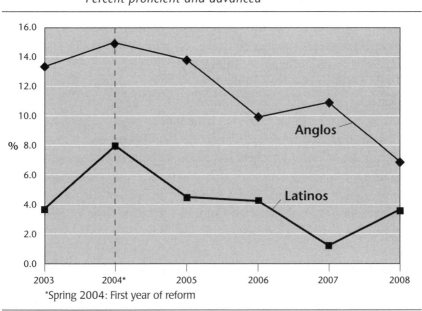

*Spring 2004: First year of reform

In contrast to the findings summarized above, the district did find some positive trends in the early years that gave rise to cautious optimism. Specific schools showed some progress in some content areas. In 2006, district analyses of CSAP showed increased scores among those students performing at proficient and advanced levels. The number of *no* scores—students who don't take the tests are given a grade of zero—dropped after implementation of small schools. Across all CSAP exams, students at some grade levels showed improvement over previous years. On the MAPS (Managed Assessment Portfolio System) test, which is more precise than CSAP and correlates highly with CSAP, administrators found that the gap between Mapleton students and their peers across the country had narrowed slightly.

ACT SCORES

Students in Colorado take the CSAP exam every year until they complete tenth grade. In eleventh grade, they all take the ACT, the most widely administered college entrance exam nationwide. The ACT is a much more precise instrument than CSAP.

While Mapleton's scores on the CSAP have not improved overall since implementation of small school reform, the ACT tells a different story. Test results from 2002 through 2007 all have similar profiles: scores drop after 2001, then begin rising after 2005. Scores in 2007 are higher in each subject area than in 2001. This held for 2008, with the notable exception that Mapleton's average reading score dropped from 16.4 to 14.4, reversing an otherwise rising trend. Figure 5.5 compares the composite scores of Mapleton students with those of all Colorado students from 2001 to 2008.

FIGURE 5.5 Mapleton eleventh graders' composite ACT scores, 2001–08

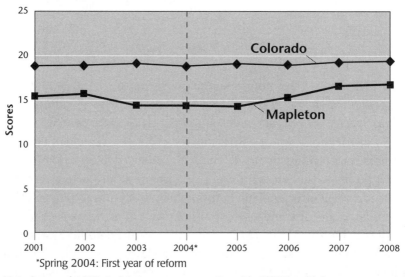

*Spring 2004: First year of reform

Note: Range of ACT is 1–36. Average score nationwide (2007) is 21.2.

For advocates of the Mapleton reform, these results are encouraging. In 2004, when the reform began, Mapleton students' composite scores were 23.4 percent lower than those of Colorado students overall. By 2008, the gap had narrowed to 14.4 percent. Furthermore, the scores do not reflect an erratic, haphazard rise, but instead seem to describe a steady trend.

OTHER INDICATORS

Other indicators typically examined to determine the effectiveness of school reform include student retention, grades, graduation rates, attendance, and discipline statistics. Mapleton has not consistently tracked performance in these areas. Some of the reports that the district has produced combine elementary and secondary data, making it difficult to discern high school trends.

Student retention and graduation rates are difficult to track in a district like Mapleton, where families are highly mobile. Using official October counts from the Colorado Department of Education, we were able to compare the number of twelfth-graders each year from 2002 through 2008 to the number of ninth-graders four years earlier. But we cannot say how many of the seniors actually attended a Mapleton school in ninth grade and how many arrived in Mapleton later in their high school careers.[3] The data presented in figure 5.6 must be considered with this caution in mind.

The chart shows an uneven retention rate. Retention had been declining before the reform. This trend continued until 2007, but retention for the class of 2008 rises, then dips slightly for the class of 2009. It's too early to tell whether the rise in 2008 reflects a trend. Notably, the class of 2008 was the first full cohort of students to experience small schools during all of their high school years in Mapleton.

Mapleton educators were encouraged by their analyses of cumulative dropout rates. The number of dropouts from the junior to the senior class fell to 5.5 percent for seniors in the class of 2008, compared with 10 percent for the class of 2007 and 11 percent for the class of 2006.

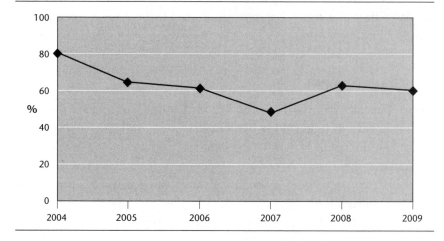

FIGURE 5.6 Mapleton senior/freshmen retention rates, 2004–09

Comparing twelfth-grade class as proportion of ninth-grade class four years earlier

But although there was some evidence of positive change, overall academic performance remained unacceptably low.

THE DISTRICT'S RESPONSE TO CSAP (2006)

The 2006 CSAP results greatly disappointed Mapleton's administrators, small school directors, teachers, and even students. Educators who were inspired by the positive outcomes on the ground—vastly improved school climate and student engagement—had hoped that their tireless efforts would be reflected in notable gains on CSAP.

By summer 2006, two of Mapleton's small high schools had completed their second year, while another four had completed their first year. Obviously, the reform was still at an early stage. But the lack of improvement in CSAP scores prompted questions about how long it would take for the new small schools to have a demonstrable effect on academic achievement. One district administrator said:

How long does it take a school to change? How long does it take to get the results that you intend to get? How long should we allow them to plan, discuss, design, and try things, before they get some kind of academic result that the state says we need and the board says we need? . . . I suppose that some would argue, "Well, it takes at least ten years to get some of those changes." . . . [But] you know, the state is saying, "I don't know how long we can wait for your CSAP scores to go up." (Morrison)

The school board remained confident that the personalization and student engagement associated with small schools would eventually—though not immediately—solve the CSAP problem. One board member recalled:

I've talked to Charlotte about that. I said, "You can't be disappointed with CSAP the first year or two. But look at individual growth among the students. You know, for the student who never came to school last year and then came to school this year, there has to be growth. But are you going to see that much growth on the CSAP tests? No, I don't think so." (Miles)

This board member felt that five years was a reasonable time in which to expect CSAP scores to rise. But Ciancio and the executive team did not believe they had five years to show improvement. The year before, the state accreditation officer, who supported the district's leadership and its dedication to reform, had nevertheless warned Mapleton that the state would intervene if CSAP scores did not go up:

I'm pretty well committed that after one more year of this—letting them get their implementation act in place—we could be moving as a state and saying no, it's not making it. And I worry about that, because I think this [reform] is very significant and very meaningful about the future of education. So I hope I don't ever have to move on them. But the reality of it is, their data is headed in the wrong direction, and most of the other districts are improving in our way of looking at them. But they're not. They're actually declining. (Phillips)

And so, in summer 2006, the district faced a critical dilemma: to what extent would it continue to adhere to the small school models, and to what extent would it impose standards-based instruction aligned with CSAP? District leaders decided to require the small schools to institute practices explicitly designed to help Mapleton students meet local and state standards.

Executive team members did not regard their decision as a major policy shift. They had believed from the start that the model developers would adapt to Mapleton as much as Mapleton adapted to them. But the tone had shifted. Now, district administrators identified content standards and certain fundamental learning principles as "nonnegotiables":

> It's a [state] mandate that kids know certain things at certain grade levels. So there should be, even in a system of small schools, some nonnegotiables, because there's movement between schools and we have some turnover of kids. And so we culled the standards in our district curriculum. Other folks [in the small schools] may call the materials they use "curriculum," but we call the actual standards documents "curriculum." We feel like those standards documents will keep us tethered to what we want kids to know and be able to do. And how schools teach kids those standards is where the uniqueness of the model comes in. (Vogel)

From the executive team's perspective, a standards-based curriculum did not compromise model fidelity, because each school would teach to the standards in its own way. Yet school directors expressed concern that the district's emphasis on CSAP would prompt a reversion to traditional instruction. The directors had always known that the litmus test of model success was improved performance on CSAP. But they had thought they would have more time to concentrate on model implementation:

> We just had a visit from our liaison to the CDE [Colorado Department of Education]. He came to our principals' meeting to say, "You

need to improve your CSAP scores." Essentially to say, "Implementing your models is all well and good, but you need better test scores and you need them now." That was his message . . . This whole thing just feels to me like completely ignoring what we're actually trying to accomplish. There wasn't much of a discussion. (Resnick)

Above all, school directors still believed in their models' capacity to boost achievement. Some staff feared that the district, attempting to strike a balance between model fidelity and standards-based instruction, was tilting too much to the latter, and that this would eventually erode each school's mission:

It's already impacted us in terms of math. We now have a math specialist who is working with every student for about 130 minutes direct each week—so, three 45-minute or three 50-minute chunks. And then he also does some small-group tutorials. That is time that is coming directly out of students' time to work on projects and students to work one-on-one with their adviser. So there's definitely a compromise to the model . . . That's a direct response to CSAP. There were just absolutely no bones about that. (Resnick)

The directors' concerns about preserving each school's distinctive character were heightened by new and revived forms of district oversight. In 2006–07, the executive team created School Support Teams (SSTs) that made monthly visits to each small school. Mapleton had deployed similar teams during a district-level accreditation process in 2001 to assure school compliance with standards-based instruction. Failing schools had been placed on a three-year watch: two years of formative and one year of summative evaluation. During the formative evaluation years, teams from the district office set up a regular schedule of school and classroom visits that gave the principals valuable feedback for improving their schools' performance. District leaders recalled that the SSTs had been effective, but they intended to improve on the original approach by having their teams operate in a less heavy-handed way. Still, for many at the school level, the expanded oversight implied a threat.[4]

SST reviews have become a formal mechanism for ensuring that each school's reform model and annual improvement plan are coordinated with district and state standards. The SST visits spur school staff to make curricular and instructional adjustments based on standardized test results, including MAPS, CSAP, and ACT, and "dashboard indicators" such as dropout statistics, disciplinary reports, and graduation figures.

The SST process strives to be collaborative, based on a common goal of helping students succeed. Yet these meetings do set policy and practice within each school and results are enforced. In fact, SST decisions are not suggestions—failure to implement can result in staff change. Certain issues at certain times can result in tense meetings, but the SSTs we observed were conducted with an air of cooperation and mutual respect. They included frank exchanges, useful information, and offers of support from district staff.

A typical SST includes one or two central administrators, possibly an educational consultant, the school director, the school's instructional guide, a lead teacher, and a parent. The director can invite students and other teachers to be part of the meeting with the team, especially the debriefing at the end of each visit. "We try to structure them so that the school's [staff and stakeholders] outnumber the central administrators. It all happens in their turf and territory." (Vogel)

Each team is assigned schools and on monthly visits collects evidence from its "walk-throughs" or "learning walks." In addition to observing classrooms and hallways, the team members talk with teachers and students. The data they gather are then shared with the director and teachers during the debriefing. In 2006–07, for example, the teams gathered data at each school on a "critical question" that had been articulated by the central administration for the entire district. For December 2006, the question was, "What are your daily walk-throughs and test data telling you about teaching and learning in your school, and what adjustments are being made to instruction based on that data?"

After each walk-through, the team convenes and the team leader completes a log sheet with the headings, "What's Working?" "Current Focus," "Challenges and Concerns," "Director's Next Steps," and "SST's Next Steps." The team's comments and observations are discussed with the director and whomever he or she has assembled to meet with the team.[5]

District administrators say that the SSTs are as committed to upholding model fidelity as they are to ensuring that standards-based teaching occurs. In short, the SST is a central office vehicle for maintaining quality control at local sites. But although the SST process is mandated by the district, the process strives to be collaborative. The visiting team calls immediate attention to both strengths and weaknesses (the word *challenges* is used in the logs). Recalling an experience at one of the schools, an executive team member highlighted an incident in which she felt that a teacher was not adhering to the model's instructional approach: "It was at an Expeditionary Learning school and . . . and it's just worksheets, packets of worksheets for these little guys. Just packets and packets of worksheets. [I asked,] 'Is that what you're about? Is that what this school is about?'" (Vogel)

Another executive team member suggested that the SSTs have improved district administrators' understanding of the different school models. This administrator also believes that the inevitable tension between district mandates and fidelity to school models is healthy:

> By being in the schools . . . [we] understand the models better than [we would] sitting up here and reading about them and hearing them tell us about them. They, by having to deal with us every month and [with] our rubrics, understand why this is important and where we are going . . . There's sometimes push-back and arguments and sometimes disagreement, and sometimes a certain amount of frustration— probably on both sides. But you have to have that if you're going to produce the tension for change. If everyone was perfectly content operating their model, or if we were perfectly content demanding that certain results occurred, we wouldn't be really changing the system. (Masterson)

Not all school directors agree that the SST visits are worthwhile, or that the district is as receptive to their concerns as the above quotations suggest. Some believe the teams are an attempt to control what they do and indicate a lack of trust. But some of the experiences related to the

SSTs turn out to be more nuanced than a stereotypical "district office versus school" characterization would suggest.

For example, one executive team member spoke of an Expeditionary Learning school whose students did poorly on the MAPS tests. The executive team member recalls meeting with the school director, who had written a draft letter to his staff about the MAPS results:

> He pulled out his letter and said, "OK, I looked at my results, and here's what I want to tell my staff, and I want you guys' opinion on this." And the letter reflected an approach . . . that was test-score focused and very inconsistent with the EL model and very inconsistent with the energy that he had created among his staff and his community and his kids. But it was based on an administrator's [concern] about his test scores going down. And so the advice at that point was, "Stop. How do you do this within your model?" not "How do you start cramming kids with CSAP information into their heads so they'll pass the test?" (Masterson)

To the executive team member, this was a case where the district *promoted* model fidelity. On the other hand, this same team member related another anecdote that revealed the district's concern about teaching to state standards. This case involved a Big Picture school:

> One of the things that we have constantly been talking with them about at the school support level is, "Where are the standards? Where are the learning outcomes? Where is the advanced thinking, as an individual student, about what you know and what you don't know and where you need to go? And why are the internships and the apprenticeships not starting with that?" They push back, understandably, and say, "Because the kid has to have a passion." We're into the passion. Great. [But] they've got these things they need to learn . . . So, how does that conversation happen? And so the push-back is the other way—about, "Where is the accountability?" (Masterson)

Certainly a tension has arisen between district administrators looking for certain constants in the curriculum, and school directors who believe that their school models and philosophies resist standardization. District administrators themselves wrestle with how to reconcile standards-driven education and constructivist principles. The SST visits have triggered open debates, so the issue is not abstract. A controversy over how to approach math instruction provides an illustrative example.

Math is the area in which Mapleton students have received the lowest scores. In fact, the percentage of students demonstrating proficiency in math steadily declined—from 11 percent to 5 percent—between 2004 and 2008. The executive team created a committee to make recommendations on how math should be taught districtwide. High school directors and teachers have resisted this approach. One executive team member explains:

> One of our strongest opponents is . . . a math teacher at Big Picture. He's like, "You do this, plus you buy us a set of materials districtwide, and you're going to kill our model." And so at the same time, on that same day, Charlotte had rolled out an article from the Big Picture Company about how Big Picture schools are closing down around the nation, because districts are imposing their standards-based practices and all their accountability measures on Big Picture and it's just ruining the model. So that day, we had an executive retreat. I'm like, "I don't know what to do with [that] high school. I don't want to be that person that shuts down that model, because I really believe in it." But our achievement in math is so dismal that if we don't really identify what we want kids to know and be able to do, and we're not really clear on that and we don't test for it, how are we going to [show any progress]? (Vogel)

Inevitably, compromises are struck that blend student-centered, constructivist approaches with content-driven state standards. The Big Picture school has found ways to integrate direct instruction into its internships. At MESA, the director acknowledges that he operates a "hybrid" school, which is not Expeditionary Learning and not a traditional, standards-based school. "We have a Mapleton Expeditionary Learning school," he says, "that is taking all of the best work and practices from EL and still upholding the standards that the state holds our kids responsible for."

Although the directors would prefer to assess learning in the ways that their models recommend, they realize that state tests are an unavoidable reality: "We're very intensely using the MAPS data . . . The kids with their parents have set a goal for increasing their score when they take [CSAP] in January and then when they take it in May. So, every ninth- and tenth-grader in this building is aware of their MAPS scores and aware of their deficits and aware of a plan for how they can improve those scores." (Taylor)

In addition, the school's ninth-grade adviser goes over the CSAP scores with her students, and the school is providing CSAP test prep. "We're going to break it down," the director said, "and we're going to help them."

GOOD REASONS FOR POOR RESULTS

The comparatively low test scores may seem puzzling, since some teachers clearly credited the small school reform with improving teaching and learning in Mapleton: "If people who read this book were thinking about becoming a small school, I would want them to know that it's a lot better than it was. We are really much more focused on academics than we were—even though our CSAP scores do not support us yet." (Fulbright)

If school climate improved and students were more engaged, why didn't CSAP scores go up? Of course, it's possible that the theory of change embedded in the reform strategy is flawed—a conclusion that critics quickly jump to. But even with a sound theory of change, a first-rate strategy, and thorough implementation, test results might not improve, at least initially. There are several legitimate reasons that this could be the case. And these reasons are worth exploring, since they have implications not only for Mapleton, but also for other districts in Colorado and nationwide.

1. The reform needs more time to have an impact on academic achievement.

It was unreasonable to expect dramatic change in the early years of implementation. After all, it would take a few years for teachers to adjust to the new curriculum and instructional demands, and for students to learn to meet the new expectations placed on them. And of course, students who have lagged in their achievement for years cannot be expected to "catch up" in a single year, no matter how promising the reform. In addition, models imported from other states promoted curricula that were not aligned to Colorado state standards. Everyone, including district administrators, teachers, and even state officials, understood that the results of the reform might not accrue immediately. But no one knew how long it might take for the reform to bring about an increase in CSAP scores.

2. Mapleton may have experienced an "implementation dip."

In districts undergoing systemic reform, it is not uncommon for achievement scores to fall and then rise, like a stunt plane after a fancy maneuver. In such cases, most education professionals would favor continuing with a reform, even though it means a tense—and politically risky— wait. Eleventh-graders' improved ACT scores may be evidence of the rise that follows an implementation dip. In tenth-grade CSAP scores, however, Mapleton has not yet seen an upswing.

Students take CSAP every year from third grade through tenth grade, and district administrators do find evidence of improvement at some grade levels. Lately, they are encouraged by initial data from "growth model" assessments, based on individual student scores across years (as opposed to aggregated grade-level scores that do not track the progress of individual students). Calculating individual growth has only recently been made possible by the state's creation of unique student identifiers that allow educators to track the progress of students over time, even if they change schools, so long as they remain in Colorado. Thus far, however, there are no dramatic gains. Professionals within and outside the district cannot say how long the wait will (or should) be for compelling evidence that innovations in school climate and student engagement are lifting achievement scores.

3. Although students are improving, their academic performance remains below grade level, so that CSAP (a psychometrically

limited instrument) cannot detect the growth that has occurred.

In his Year Two (2007) evaluation, Kevin Welner quotes an administrator questioning teachers' expectations of student work:

> I'm not seeing the level of rigor that we expect in any of our schools. None of 'em. I never have . . . I've seen more engagement by kids. I'm seeing more attention to kids and among kids. I'm seeing more production from kids. [But] I'm not seeing a level of expectation from kids that I think is high school level. I'm seeing probably seventh-grade work in tenth-grade classrooms, and that's got to stop.[6]

Some teachers might agree with this assessment. Yet teachers who believe that students are fully capable of *reaching* grade-level expectations can be emphatic in pointing out that many students *enter* high school with skills far below grade level.

It is a principle of school reform, and of education practice generally, that you meet students where they are. Mapleton teachers tell us that their high school students come to them with reading and math skills as low as third-grade level. How can a teacher hold a tenth-grader to expectations of tenth-grade work when the student reads, writes, and performs math at the third- or sixth- or eighth-grade level? If a fifteen-year-old is reading at the seventh-grade level, expecting tenth-grade work from him would be no different than expecting it from a twelve-year-old actually enrolled in the seventh grade. You can call the student lazy, hold firm to your expectations, and watch that student fail and possibly drop out—as do approximately half the students enrolled in urban school districts nationwide. Or you can provide instruction that meets students where they are, hoping to keep them motivated and challenged enough that they will rise to grade level as quickly as possible.

Mapleton is hardly unique in this respect. Test results from other urban districts—including San Francisco, Los Angeles, Boston, Houston, and Washington, D.C.—all tell the same story: the *majority* of high school students do not meet grade-level expectations, and many perform several grade levels below where they should be. Therefore, as disheartening as it is to find fifth-grade work in tenth-grade classrooms, it is no solution merely to declare, "That's got to stop."

These considerations come into play when we try to interpret the results of CSAP and other standardized state tests. All such tests are calibrated to specific grade-level expectations. They measure only whether a student is performing at the grade level in which the student is enrolled. As a result, students will not begin to show increased scores on such tests until they advance into the cognitive range for which the tests were designed.

Imagine a tall building with exactly one window, nine stories up. This represents the ninth-grade CSAP exam. Looking out the window of the building is a test administrator with an award. The administrator will give the award to any child who appears within his field of vision. The award signifies ninth-grade proficiency.

Against the building are several ladders of varying heights, ranging from three stories high all the way to eleven stories. The student who climbs to the third story will not get an award, because he obviously will not be visible to the test administrator. The student who climbs twice that, to six stories, will also not be seen. The student who climbs to the eighth story might come partially into view. That student will get the "Partially Proficient" award. But students who climb from, say, the third story all the way to the seventh story in one year will be just as invisible to the test administrator as the students who begin at the third story and stay there, or who take the entire year to reach the fourth story.

Based on students' CSAP scores (how high up the building students climb), test administrators place groups of students into categories: *Unsatisfactory*, *Partially Proficient*, *Proficient*, and *Advanced*. Within these categories, students are distributed along a continuum of scores. But the CSAP and other similar state tests are not very precise at the low and high ends. For example, CSAP cannot accurately distinguish between a student performing several years below grade level and a student performing just two years below grade level: both will score in the "Unsatisfactory" range, but their scores may not reliably reflect their different levels of performance. This is why, in Colorado, it is illegal to use CSAP for diagnostic purposes.

This is not necessarily a weakness of CSAP. Like most standards-driven state tests, CSAP was not designed to determine the grade level at which a student is performing. Rather, it was designed to determine whether a student is meeting expectations for a specific grade level. With respect to Mapleton, CSAP scores tell us that large numbers of students are falling outside the Proficient range, and this is clearly a legitimate cause for concern. But it may be that students are climbing higher ladders now than they were before the reform was implemented. If that is the case, CSAP may not be a sufficiently sensitive instrument to detect their elevated performance.

4. The logic model that Mapleton leaders rely on may not be borne out in practice.

According to the logic model at the heart of the Mapleton reform, smaller schools and relevant curricula engage students, engaged students work harder and become invested in their learning, and as a result, they stay in school and achievement goes up. Yet as we observed in chapter 2, research has not confirmed the links between altered school environments, student engagement, and achievement. In any case, the links do not appear to be inevitable.

Early data about academic outcomes following the Mapleton reform do not tell a consistent story. While CSAP proficiency rates remained stagnant or fell, ACT scores rose. ACT is a more accurate test than CSAP, but is administered only to eleventh-graders. Moreover, as we have seen, CSAP proficiency rates may not have captured achievement gains among students who were not yet functioning at grade level. Faced with conflicting or inconclusive data, evaluators cannot make definitive judgments about a reform's effectiveness. Yet conflicting data, especially in a reform's early years, are more common than data that uniformly point to success or failure.

Here we see another inevitable dilemma of school reform. In today's political climate, scores on state tests are often taken as the clear measure of whether a reform is working. But the pressure for tangible achievement gains is likely to rise more quickly than test scores do. Proponents may argue that a reform is having positive effects that show up unevenly, or not at all, on the state tests; they may point to other indicators—such as attendance, discipline records, grades, and increased graduation rates—as evidence that a reform is achieving desirable outcomes. Nonetheless, it is almost impossible to shift the public focus away from test scores.

Even so, the apparent numerical precision of test score data can be misleading. Within the volumes of output that test data generate, trends and nuances can yield any number of stories. If one asked several meteorologists to summarize the weather in the United States for any given day, a range of reports might be submitted, ranging from *miserable* to *fair* to *outstanding*, even if the thermometers and wind gauges were perfectly calibrated. Analyses of test data work similarly, although instrument quality varies.

Some observers clearly have unrealistic notions about what it takes to raise test scores appreciably, especially when students begin each academic year far below grade level, as most do in urban high schools. Under common conditions, motivated students engaged in the most challenging of curricula can improve their performance by one and one-half grade levels in an academic year. There are schools that have boosted student performance a few grade levels in a year, and this is heartening. But it is also uncommon. If students improve at a rate of one and one-half grade levels each year, those who enter ninth grade performing below seventh-grade level might achieve grade-level proficiency before graduating as seniors. But they are unlikely to show proficiency on CSAP, which is administered only until the tenth grade.

In the absence of skyrocketing test scores, other measures can be used to track a reform's progress. Mapleton administrators were generous in responding to our requests for data. Yet Mapleton and other districts engaged in school reform often struggle to provide continuous and fine-grained data on indicators such as retention, participation in extracurricular activities, teacher turnover, student acceptance into college, escalating or diminishing discipline reports, attendance, and grade point averages. Such indicators may shift before test scores do and can become the basis for compelling arguments to extend or modify a reform.

ACCURATE ESTIMATES AND OBJECTIVE OPINIONS: TWO OXYMORONS OF SCHOOL REFORM

"Truth, after all, wears a different face to everybody, and it would be too tedious to wait till all were agreed."
—James Russell Lowell

The release of the CSAP data in 2006 prompted a shift in the rhetoric and focus of implementation. Fidelity to each school's model became subordinate to the district's push for standards-based instruction that would (it was hoped) raise test scores. Several district administrators argue that this push was an inevitable part of the reform, to be launched once the small schools were established. Clearly, however, the shift in emphasis was also a response to the CSAP results and to the pressure the district was facing from the state and disappointed parents. In a standards-driven policy environment, if test scores do not go up, reforms risk being supplanted by traditional approaches. Reversion to the familiar occurs even though failure to improve using such methods is often the motivation to implement reform in the first place.

Some of the school directors and teachers, who were pleased about advances in school climate and student engagement, felt that newly imposed district curriculum standards, demands for direct instruction in math, and frequent SST visits eroded their models and threatened to drive the schools back towards traditional instruction. For some directors, the notion of model integrity was categorical—you have it or you don't. Others recognized degrees of model fidelity and were trying to find their place along a continuum. In our review of SST logs, we discerned some movement away from single-minded commitment to a particular reform model. District administrators believed that the schools could take measures to raise CSAP scores without compromising the models. But how much could the district intervene without jeopardizing curricular relevance, student-centered instruction, and differentiation—elements at the heart of the small school reform?

As we noted in chapter 3, when Mapleton educators addressed logistical issues during the start-up year (i.e., how to schedule sports practices for students from several schools), they had to make trade-offs between school autonomy and district control. On these issues, discussions were amicable and compromises, with some exceptions, easily negotiated. But issues of curriculum and instruction ignited passions. Some school directors, who were expressly hired because of their commitment to the principles of the reform, and who in turn had hired teachers who embraced those principles, resisted what they perceived as a change of course and a threat to the school cultures they had been working to create. District administrators, on the other hand, felt that it was unrealistic for school directors to think that the district would not be deeply involved in curriculum and instruction. They also felt they had made it clear from the beginning that their involvement would be ongoing.

In most cases, the periodic SST visits have moderated the tensions between school directors and central administrators. District staff have provided both resources and expertise to help directors and teachers link their curricula to state standards without sacrificing the heart and soul of each model. They have also provided directors with leverage to bring about school-level changes. As a result, a climate of collaboration has gradually developed. By 2009, school leaders and staff, as well as district administrators, saw that ideological loyalty could work against the best interests of students. When student needs became the focus, tensions about model fidelity diminished.

We believe that the choice between model fidelity and curricular standardization poses an inevitable, intractable dilemma for small school reform. Even though most of the power lies on the district's side, tensions in Mapleton were moderated to the extent that district administrators themselves were committed to model fidelity. Moreover, in Mapleton, as in most districts, people recognized that students and teachers are better served by collaboration than by confrontation. Knowing this, however, didn't make discussions and negotiations easy. In other districts, where goodwill between school- and district-level staff may be shaky at best, tensions of the kind we are examining here can mean the end of reform.

Another tension over accountability has worried small school advocates. They say that current accountability systems have led to a narrowing of educational objectives. Educators nationwide have voiced concerns about the focus on student performance on standardized tests. They argue that such a focus preempts other legitimate aims of schooling, including civic education, psychosocial development, and cultivation of students' talents and interests in the visual arts, music, and even sports.

And yet, when people read questions from CSAP and similar assessments, they tend to think that students *should* be able to demonstrate proficiency on these tests. CSAP is no college entrance exam; the questions reflect expectations for basic skill development at each grade level. We believe that CSAP does measure what it claims to measure, and that if students can't perform well on CSAP, they aren't performing at grade level. And though we do not believe that other legitimate outcomes of education ought to be treated as peripheral to academic achievement, they cannot substitute for it, either.

Evidence will be found across a range of data—even within the same data set—to support the positions of those who favor the reform and those who don't. Mapleton staff believe that the data indicate halting but nevertheless inexorable progress, which they interpret as validation of the logic model. But they will need to convince parents and community leaders, the school board, and the Colorado Department of Education. The perceptions of these key stakeholders will greatly influence the extent to which small schools in Mapleton prove to be a sustainable reform.

CHAPTER SIX

Sustaining the Reform

In previous chapters, we have examined the history and context of small school reform in Mapleton, analyzed the principles undergirding the reform, described the process of implementation, and asked whether the reform has met its stated objectives. In this chapter, we address the question: Is the reform sustainable?

In any school district, a combination of internal factors—political, logistical, and financial—can strengthen, compromise, or end a reform. Some reforms depend on a single individual, most often the superintendent. Think of David Hornbeck in Philadelphia in the 1990s or Gerry House in Memphis in the early 2000s. When these leaders left their posts, the reforms they sought to implement were abandoned by their successors. External factors, including pressures from state legislatures and policy makers, can also determine the fate of a reform. In Colorado, the demand for improved test scores has placed Mapleton's efforts under heightened scrutiny. Thus far, however, state officials have been willing to give the small schools time to demonstrate their effectiveness. Therefore, the sustainability of Mapleton's reform mainly depends, for now, on three factors within the district:

- *No reform as extensive as Mapleton's can survive unless it is institutionalized at the district level.* The superintendent and executive committee must retain the school board's support for their reform agenda and ensure that community groups remain fully informed about any changes in either reform direction or substance. They must recruit new district leaders and central staff who understand the rationale for small schools and share in the spirit of the reform, even though they were not involved in its implementation. As a matter of policy, district officials must evaluate practices and facilities in light of the reform's needs and objectives, recognizing that some apparent inefficiencies may be necessary accommodations to a small school reform based on choice.

- *The reform must be sustained at the school level.* Factors such as teacher and principal turnover, institutional inertia, and a gradual diminution of energy and commitment render many reforms temporary. In Mapleton, each small school faces the challenge of retaining its distinctive identity as an Expeditionary Learning school, a Big Picture school, a New Technology school, and so on, rather than reverting to traditional structures and curricula and homogenizing over time.

- *The reform must be financially viable.* Early on in the new wave of small school reform, enthusiastic promoters promised that, after start-up, the operating costs of small schools would be no greater than those of comprehensive high schools. This was counterintuitive to many educators, since large schools enjoy economies of scale that are unavailable to small schools. Still, advocates argued that since the small schools they envisioned would have the same teacher-student ratios as large schools and fewer administrators (per school), per-pupil costs would not change. In this chapter, we present data examining the operating costs of small schools in Mapleton.

PRESERVING SMALL SCHOOL REFORM AT THE DISTRICT LEVEL

Charlotte Ciancio has been fortunate in having an extremely support-ive school board since she was hired in 2001. Board members trusted her and shared her ideals, and they have enthusiastically endorsed each step of the reform. Moreover, board turnover since 2001 has only reinforced Ciancio's leadership. Even though none of the members who hired Ciancio are still in place (some seats have turned over twice), the board remains both supportive and cohesive. Ciancio commented: "They don't fight about anything. I've never had a fight from the board, never . . . They discuss issues all the time, [but] they raise the issue as a question, not as a position. I don't think I have any board members who are positional."

As pressure mounts for higher test scores, or as new board members bring alternative perspectives, Ciancio could lose some of the autonomy she currently enjoys. Still, she thinks it is unlikely that the board would seek to change course entirely: "[A]s we've redesigned our schools, we've really taken on the cry that we've heard on the West Coast—of going so far you can't go back. And so, when you go that far to make your comprehensive high school no longer look or feel like a comprehensive high school, then you may not be tempted to go back into a comprehensive high school."

District leaders are aware that sustaining the reform will require central administrators and school staff who understand and support it, even if they weren't involved in the initial implementation. At the district level, new staff often come from the small schools. In some cases, people are promoted into district-level positions because of their familiarity with the reform. Other new hires learn about it from Mapleton's recruiting materials.

The district must also develop a physical infrastructure to sustain the reform. In November 2007, Ciancio and her executive team presented two ballot initiatives to Mapleton voters. One would have provided more funds for instruction; the district hoped to hire more teachers and thereby reduce class sizes. The other initiative would have supported capital improvements. Ciancio explained that the newest school building in Mapleton is over forty years old and that some schools "are falling apart from the inside out." The capital improvement plan included construction of two new buildings that would house three small schools. "Our vision," Ciancio said, "is to take the main campus and kind of chop it up a little bit, to make it look and feel more like a college campus would feel, with the shared facilities being the gym and the food court . . . and the auditorium. But their classroom spaces would be unique."

Ciancio sees the college campus concept as an extension of the small schools approach. Even with the shared facilities, each school would provide an intellectual "home base" for students, a smaller environment where they are known by all of the adults. Mapleton administrators believe that renovations to accommodate small school teaching and learning would enhance the delivery of the reform. But they also say that the bond initiative would be necessary in any case. Buildings need to be outfitted with fire sprinklers and security systems. Walls, foundations, and roofs need repair, and energy-saving measures must be implemented. All these renovations would be required whether small schools were in place or not. Yet the fact that the vehicle of instruction in Mapleton is small schools will influence how spaces are remodeled.

Voters, however, narrowly rejected both ballot initiatives, first in 2007 and again in 2008. The loss in 2007 was attributed to low voter turnout, especially among parents (only 2,707 votes were cast). The loss in 2008 came after a concerted drive at the district and school levels. This time, nearly 10,000 votes were cast, and each initiative lost by fewer than 800 votes. Mapleton insiders attributed the defeat to the fact that a large proportion of MPS parents are not eligible to vote and to a very powerful, eleventh-hour counter-campaign by business owners in the city.

In 2009, the superintendent said that she would place the initiatives on the ballot again, even though the parent and business communities had been hard hit by the economic downturn. In spring 2009, the Mapleton zip code had the third-highest foreclosure rate in Colorado, and the county unemployment rate was 9.4 percent, two percentage points higher than the rate for Colorado as a whole.[1] Still, Ciancio felt strongly about the need to go back to the voters, saying, "You can never really afford to raise your taxes—but you can't afford not to support your schools."

SUSTAINING REFORM AT THE SCHOOL LEVEL

Attracting and retaining teachers who are effective in a small school setting is essential to sustaining the reform. Many teachers now seek out Mapleton because of the promise of working in a small school—a fact that gives the district an advantage in its recruiting efforts. As part of the selection process, Mapleton uses a screening instrument to determine whether applicants have the personality types that do well in a small school environment. It has also created an extensive induction program, providing full-time release to experienced staff to work with first- and second-year teachers.[2]

Yet nearly one-quarter of Mapleton's secondary teachers are turning over each year, and in the initial years of implementation the figure was higher (see chapter 3). Since the reform began, Mapleton has created incentives to help reduce teacher turnover, including a bonus for completing 150 hours of professional development. In addition, it administers exit surveys to better understand why teachers leave. Ciancio acknowledged (and one model partner agreed) that during the first two years of the reform, teachers were overtaxed by the challenge of creating curriculum while starting up the new small schools. In addition, teachers nearing retirement or those who didn't want to participate in small school reform left the district. Now that curricular supports are in place, Ciancio believes that teacher retention will improve.

Mapleton's reform depends heavily on teacher retention, since most new teachers will not have been trained in the distinctive educational models promoted by each school. Nor will new teachers have benefited from the extensive professional development that accompanied initial implementation. New teachers are trained in the school models by colleagues and, to a lesser extent, model partners. Since the 2007–08 year (Year Five of implementation), schools have been funded based on a formula that takes into account teachers' years of experience; schools with younger staff receive more money for professional development. Each school retains discretion to use professional development funds as it wishes, and all small high schools still have contracts with their model partners. But unless Mapleton is able to retain teachers who understand the models and the goals of the small schools in which they teach, the reform could revert back to more traditional curriculum and instruction.[3]

Since initial implementation, all schools have acquired new leadership. As school directors change, new leaders must understand the curriculum and instruction promoted by their school's design. At the same time, Ciancio has changed what she looks for in school directors:

> I think it takes a different skill set to start a new school—[someone] with an entrepreneurial kind of attitude, who can take a design and run with it and create systems that support something different. [Those activities require] a different skill set than really drilling deep and looking forward with the learning. So I actually have a lot of shift in the leadership in all of our high schools. It takes a different kind of a leader now to really run with the ball.

In their first year, new directors who are not steeped in their school models are provided several weeks of training with model partners, at the district's expense. Beyond this, however, there are variations in how much coaching and other support directors (and teachers) receive from the model partners.

When we asked what is being done to ensure that model principles are incorporated into classroom practice, Ciancio pointed to the work of School Support Teams (SSTs), whose members include central administrators, school staff, parents, and other stakeholders. These teams make monthly visits to every classroom in every school:

> And they go through and look at, "Are you aligned with the mission that's stated?" "Are you really doing what it is you said you were going to do?" "And what are the elements that would give evidence of that?" So it's every classroom every month, a lot of dialogue, prebrief, debrief . . . Also, the design partners come and do this, and they give us feedback: "Charlotte, I'm worried about what I'm seeing," or "I'm really excited about this." So there are a lot of eyes in every classroom.

SSTs serve multiple functions. For example, the teams work out ways that the director and his or her staff can integrate state standards into the curriculum as well as respond to the model partners' advice. SSTs negotiate important changes in curriculum and instructional design. In some cases, these innovations have been adopted by model partners nationwide.

Another informal role played by the SST is to put pressure on those directors and teachers who, in the words of one SST member, "don't get it." The SST member referred to cases in which a director or teacher might not follow through on repeated directives from the SSTs. Since SST logs and conversations are public and reported to the superintendent, pressure grows that can leverage such changes. In at least three cases since 2006, school directors have exited as a result of inability or refusal to adopt practices mandated by SSTs.[4]

Thus, SSTs, both formally and informally, turn out to be the vehicle for maintaining consistency between district and school policies, as well as the mechanism by which to sustain the reform's core principles while adapting to changing circumstances.

FINANCING SMALL SCHOOLS

In August 2009, Charlotte Ciancio and her executive team asked the school board to put another capital improvements bond issue before the voters in the fall, and the school board agreed. Earlier in the summer, however, the state awarded Mapleton a $32 million matching grant, so the district was required to seek only half the amount ($30 million) it needed for capital improvements. A linked initiative sought increased funding for district operations, particularly in the area of instruction. As noted above, Ciancio has said that she would have sought both ballot initiatives even if small school reform had never taken place. Still, and despite the early claims of small school advocates, administrators have found that many operating costs for small schools are indeed higher than they are for comprehensive schools, mostly because of lost economies of scale in purchasing and increased demands on facilities.

With the help of Mapleton administrators, we have analyzed budget trends in the district, using data from FY2003–08. To understand the budgetary impact of the small schools, we analyzed per-pupil expenditures for each year, and how much of per-pupil allotments went to various costs. As a first step, we grouped the district's operating costs into five categories:

- *Instruction:* Includes any interaction between students and teachers, paraprofessionals, or aides. This category includes classroom instruction, distance learning, and in-home support.

- *Student Support:* Includes curriculum development, staff training, library services, and supervision of special education, vocational, and athletic programs and services. It also includes activities that promote the health and well-being of students, including counseling and health services, audiology, and occupational and physical therapy.

- *General Administration:* Includes the formation and implementation of district and state policy, legal services, elections, human resources, superintendent activities, and community relations.

- *Site Operations:* Includes activities related to school administration, including director activities, maintenance of school records, and clerical support, as well as operations and maintenance of buildings and vehicles, groundskeeping, and transportation of students.

- *Central Services:* Includes police services, research, data analysis and evaluation, communication services, public information services, staff services, risk management, and telecommunication services.

Funding formulas in Colorado call for increased per-pupil allotments each year to help keep up with inflation, so we could not compare years by looking strictly at dollars spent in each category. However, we could make meaningful comparisons by looking at the proportions of the district budget devoted to various categories of expenditure from year to year. Since state law requires districts to balance their budgets, we knew that increases in some categories would have to be offset by reductions in others. We therefore asked: "Over the period FY2003–08, which spending categories increased or decreased as a proportion of total per-pupil expenditure?"

In FY2007 (this would be the academic year 2007–08, the fifth year of implementation), 5 percent of the district's overall operating costs—$2 million out of $40 million—were directly attributable to the small school reform. During this period, spending in two categories—Site Operations and Central Operations—increased as a proportion of total per-pupil expenditures. To help offset these increases, spending in another category—Instruction—decreased as a proportion of total per-pupil expenditures. By FY2008, however, costs began to stabilize. At that point, external funding for implementation had ended, so operating expenses were borne nearly entirely by the district.

Figure 6.1 presents spending in each category for FY2003–08. In FY2008, the proportion of per-pupil expenditures devoted to Instruction

FIGURE 6.1   **District spending as proportion of per-pupil expenditures by category, 2003–2008**

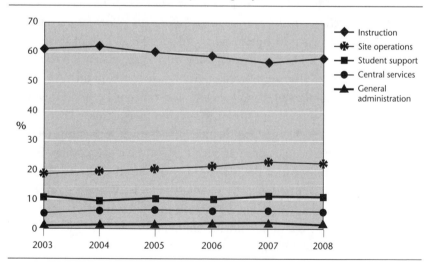

rose slightly after several years of decline. Student Support, which had been fluctuating between 10 percent and 11 percent since implementation, was at 11 percent. General Administration accounted for just 2 percent of per-pupil expenditures; this figure has remained unchanged since FY2003. Site Operations, which in FY2003 accounted for 19 percent of per-pupil expenditures, climbed steadily and reached 23 percent in FY2008. This increase—the greatest change in district spending in any category—is analyzed in more detail below. Central Services increased from 6 to 7 percent of per-pupil expenditures between FY2003 and FY2007, but declined back to 6 percent in FY2008. Many of these costs were borne by the Gates Foundation implementation grant, which ended in FY2007.

Since Site Operations seems to have been affected most by the small school reform, we subjected this category to additional analysis. Site Operations comprises school administration, student transportation, and operations and maintenance. In FY2003, school administration and student transportation accounted for 47 percent of Site Operations expenditures. By FY2007, each had increased its share by 2 percent, raising the figure to 51 percent. Examining the components of Site Operations in more detail, we noted the following trends:

- *From 2003 to 2007, school administration costs increased 55 percent relative to what they were before the reform.* Given that the district was now operating six to seven high schools instead of one, this is no surprise. At one time during the transition to small schools, Mapleton supported eight high school administrators— twice the number of principals and assistants as before. However, many of these positions are now covered by existing FTE, which has not changed, so the net increase in administration costs has not been as dramatic as it might have been otherwise. Furthermore, most of the increased costs for administrative personnel aren't tied directly to small schools. When the reform started, Mapleton's policy was to allot an extra administrator for every four hundred students eligible for free or reduced-price lunch (FRL). Such eligibility is a proxy for poverty. It became clear, however, that the number of administrators assigned on the basis of that ratio wouldn't effectively address students' needs, so the ratio was revised, resulting in greater administrative costs. In addition, at the beginning of the reform, the average percentage of FRL students at the high school level was 50 percent. By 2008–09, the figure had risen to 63 percent, with further increases projected in subsequent years.

- *Student transportation costs increased 73 percent.* As we saw in chapter 3, the Mapleton reform required the district to transport each child to his or her school of choice.

- *Operations and maintenance costs increased 33 percent.* This increase mainly reflects utility costs: the district was heating and cooling more buildings than before, even as fuel and electricity rates rose nationally.

The trend line for spending on Instruction was very different. Conversion to small schools brought an initial cost saving of 5 percent in teacher salaries, as experienced teachers retired or transferred to other districts. (Of course, as the new teachers who replaced them move up the pay scale in coming years, Instruction costs will increase accordingly.) The proportion of per-pupil expenditures devoted to Instruction decreased from 61 percent in FY2003 to 57 percent in FY2007. In FY2008, however, the figure rose to 58 percent. District administrators believe that this increase will be the start of a trend.

Today, the district has balanced its budget, in part, by reducing staff development to the minimum required by state law. Implementation of a K–12 reading program adopted by the district in FY2008 was facilitated by asking teachers to volunteer for training. All but five teachers districtwide agreed to participate. District administrators say that if they had more money, they would fund more paraprofessionals and other student support positions. Those positions could be purchased currently through offsets to other categories—Site Operations, for example. Yet doing so would dilute the district's mission and threaten the reform.

Capital expenditures are not reflected in the figures discussed above. Although Mapleton owned the buildings that would house the small schools, some of these buildings had to be renovated to accommodate them. In addition, given the accelerated pace of the reform, the renovations had to be done quickly, so the district took out loans to ensure timely completion. Interest payments on these loans have added to the reform's cost.

Currently, funds that might otherwise have been shifted into the district's capital reserves are being used for operating expenses. As a result, the capital reserve account has a minimal balance, limiting the district's ability to pay for site improvements, including major repairs to roofs and plumbing, sprinklers, and security cameras. In addition, funds for capital equipment such as copy machines, duplicators, science equipment, and computers are "severely limited." With buildings forty to fifty years old, district facilities would need remodeling and retrofitting even if small school reform had not been implemented.

Mapleton's experience is both unique and generic. Implementation of small schools will inevitably increase a district's operating costs. But the specific circumstances in each district will determine where those costs will accrue and how they will be absorbed. In Mapleton, the mission statement promised an "enticing menu of learning opportunities." To make this menu genuinely available, transportation had to be provided so that all students could access all schools. This is one of the significant costs of Mapleton's reform. Other districts that have subways or more extensive public bus systems, for example, might not face the transportation issues that Mapleton did, but might require building purchases or remodeling or some other expense that would have to be offset elsewhere.

Thus, while small school reform is bound to increase a district's operating costs, its precise budgetary impact is impossible to predict. To Mapleton's chief budget officer, this is one lesson of the reform:

I'd love to be able to say [that the measures we took to balance the budget] were a result of exhaustive, detailed planning and we knew it would happen this way. But in reality, there was a tremendous amount of trial-and-error that went on. We anticipated where we could, but there was so much we didn't and couldn't know. When you eliminate attendance boundaries, how do you know which population of kids would enroll where? How was transportation going to shake out with family choices? If we take the old building out of mothballs, how can we anticipate utility and maintenance costs? (Henley)

Some advocates for small schools believe that the costs of reform should be calculated per graduate, not per student. Under this accounting scheme, small schools, if indeed they increase retention and graduation rates, might be judged more economical than large, comprehensive high schools. The chief budget officer appreciates the thinking behind this proposal:

I like the idea of analysis based on graduates. People are always saying, "Couldn't you save money by going back to one big high school? Or, for that matter, why not just merge with a neighboring district?" Well, we could. The data show that. If you want to think of a school as a big factory, then sure, the bigger the better. But we tried the factory model, and it doesn't produce cars that run. So what's the point, exactly? You can pretend you're accomplishing something and feel good about the money you're "saving." But in reality, you're just shoveling money into a ditch. Unless you're producing graduates who are prepared to "achieve their dreams," you've just wasted thirteen years of their life. (Henley)

Yet public education administrators do not have the luxury of securing funds based on cost-benefit analyses or of amortizing instructional costs over decades. In public schooling, revenues are based on enrollment and operating expenses must be managed on an annual basis. Administrators have to manage small schools within existing revenue constraints. Implementing small school reform involves trade-offs that have very real financial and operational consequences.

LESSONS LEARNED

Over the past several years, small school reform in the United States has completed a predictable trajectory. Beginning with the promise of dramatic change and the infusion of millions of dollars into districts across the country, the reform has advanced to the more mundane yet equally critical phase of stabilizing and sustaining new programs and approaches. In any district, sustaining reform depends on the commitment and support of the superintendent and executive team, the school board, a critical mass of school staff and district personnel, and the community. For the most part, these essential elements have been in place in Mapleton. But the rejection of ballot initiatives in two recent elections gives cause for concern.

Ciancio did not see the failed initiatives as votes against small schools. She believed that parents supported the reform and that the district could sway business owners who opposed an increase in their taxes. By the time this book is published, the 2009 election will have shown whether she was correct.

For the hundreds of small, urban districts across the nation, Mapleton's experience in putting its reforms into practice offers several useful lessons. To be sure, Mapleton had (and has) features unlikely to be replicated elsewhere (i.e., a home-grown superintendent who has stayed in the post more than eight years, an initial budget surplus, and stakeholders aching for a new page to be turned in school reform). But just as surely, Mapleton faced imperatives and challenges that other districts are certain to encounter as well. This is why the Mapleton story should prove instructive for school boards and superintendents considering, launching, or persevering through the early years of small school reform.

Lesson 1: Secure Community Support

Educators embarking on the kind of extensive reform that Mapleton undertook must gauge the political climate carefully and ensure that parent and community support are wide and deep. Community disapproval can sway state officials and kill ballot initiatives necessary to sustain a reform. Moreover, superintendents and school boards must be aligned; otherwise, potent internal and external pressures can generate resistance and make reform impossible.

Lesson 2: Preserve the Principles of the Reform Models

For district leaders and school directors committed to altering traditional classroom practices and producing gains in state test scores, preserving the design principles of whole school reform models will remain a significant challenge.

In an era of strict accountability, the sustainability of reforms ultimately depends on whether they produce demonstrable gains in students' test scores. As we noted in chapter 5, a school reform may yield improvements that aren't immediately discernible in test scores. Unfortunately, political pressures at all levels are reducing the acceptable "wait time" for results. While these pressures do militate against complacency, they also risk ending or compromising reforms that might be working, especially constructivist-based ones, where the link between learning process and testing achievement is less obvious than it is for more traditional instruction.

In Mapleton, negotiating the dilemma of producing tangible results versus honoring the principles of the reform models has resulted in a standards-based curriculum delivered through a combination of traditional and constructivist classroom practices. Educators will recognize the compromises implied in that statement. But without these compromises, it is unlikely that the reform would have survived. Yet every compromise was carefully deliberated and weighed against the mission statement. While policies and practices in Mapleton are continually modified, the mission statement has not been compromised.

Lesson 3: Anticipate Increased Operating Costs

Districts contemplating small school reform should anticipate increased operating costs that may not be covered by grants, especially after initial implementation. Our analysis shows that small schools increased

Mapleton's operating costs by 5 percent, requiring shifts in other budget items. To keep its budget in balance, the district has reduced spending on instruction as a proportion of total per-pupil expenditures and drawn down its capital reserves. District administrators believe that they could not increase funding for instruction and capital reserves without compromising the mission.

When a reform is mission driven, a district will have to make real trade-offs in balancing its budget. The sustainability of small school reform depends in part on whether schools and districts can live with these trade-offs. In some districts, for example, small schools have eliminated many of the extracurricular activities that comprehensive high schools once provided, such as sports and band. However, cutting—or even reducing—these programs is highly unpopular among students and community members. Many schools and districts have proud traditions in sports, drama, and music, the elimination of which can erode support for the reform overall. In Mapleton, the district has strived to maintain these activities. For this reason, it has not used reductions in spending on extracurricular programs as an offset for the costs of small school implementation.

Our analysis of expenditures in Mapleton is not definitive. We have not seen extensive, thoughtful projections of the real costs of implementing small school reform as compared with the costs of continuing to operate large, comprehensive high schools. Districts that have implemented small schools need to share their experiences in balancing their operating and capital budgets. In what categories have cost increases occurred, what has been the magnitude of those costs, and what trade-offs have been made to cover them? The integrity of school reform demands that these and other fiscal questions be asked. The sustainability of reforms may depend on the answers.

Lesson 4: Manage the Inevitable Dilemmas of Reform

Inescapable dilemmas accompany small school reforms. As we have seen, such dilemmas arise even in districts with the most thoughtful, motivated, and energetic school and central staff. District leaders who ignore, deny, underestimate, or fear these dilemmas place their reforms at risk. Consider these examples from the Mapleton experience:

Moving ahead quickly to take advantage of a window of support versus obtaining buy-in from stakeholders. The pace of implementation will depend on political and financial factors. The faster the implementation, the greater the risk of failing to secure participation and understanding from critical stakeholders. Seeing that conditions were favorable for an ambitious reform, Mapleton administrators took the calculated risk of opening seven small schools in three years. To effect this, district and school administrators were encouraged to alter or abandon long-standing policies and procedures and to institute changes that supported the ideals of the small school reform. For district administrators, school directors, teachers, and students who were accustomed to "business as usual," the scale and pace of reform were sometimes unsettling.

When changes come too quickly or abruptly, they can undermine district and school leaders' credibility and authority. Yet, at times, such changes are essential to overcome inertia and preserve a reform's integrity. In other districts, conditions may be more favorable to a slower pace. But a gradual approach increases the risk that changes in school board membership, interventions in the policy arena, or unexpected events will interrupt or sideline planning or implementation.

Decentralizing authority versus satisfying demands for consistency, accountability, and fiscal equity that are characteristic of school districts. The rhetoric of small school reform places responsibility on school staff for budgeting, scheduling, curriculum, and student advising. Yet the hierarchy of public schooling places ultimate responsibility for school success on district leadership. In a small school reform, district leaders must continually balance their legal and administrative accountability with demands for school site control.

This dilemma manifested itself in various ways throughout the Mapleton reform. Whereas "autonomy" is a core value of the small school movement, Charlotte Ciancio insisted that the operative term in

Mapleton was "agency." School staff would have the freedom to make certain decisions, but they could not function independently of the district. Even within this framework, however, tensions between school- and district-level authority were unavoidable. The dilemma continues to play out, but negotiated compromises over these conflicting values have become routine over time. The SST meetings, as well as discussions about budget authority granted to small schools, have become forums in which give-and-take between schools and the district can take place. While certain autonomies are recognized as legitimate areas to negotiate (e.g., instructional approach, textbook adoption), others are understood to be nonnegotiable (e.g., operating expenses, per-pupil expenditures, and, most important, state curricular standards). Issues continue to arise that don't clearly fall into the "negotiable" or "nonnegotiable" category, but so far, SSTs, the budgeting system, and union contract talks have provided forums for working out these issues.

Staying the course versus making necessary adjustments. Rarely will a reform be implemented without modification and then left untouched. One of the most difficult aspects of implementing a reform, especially one as extensive as Mapleton's, is determining whether it is working and how to respond to early indications of its impact. Test scores provide deceptively authoritative data, but tests—especially state tests—are not precise instruments and rarely yield conclusive results. Other measures are no less flawed and may yield contradictory assessments of a reform's success. For this reason, judgments about whether a reform is working, how, and for whom, are necessarily subjective, at least in the early years of implementation.

In response to test scores and other data, and in the face of political pressure within and outside the system, educators often make midcourse corrections. In Mapleton's case, the district implemented math curricula and oversight of classroom instruction through SSTs. Inevitably, there was much debate about whether these midcourse corrections were strengthening or subverting the reform. This dilemma persists at Mapleton, as it inevitably will in other districts that have undergone major reform. Successfully anticipating and negotiating this dilemma can mean the difference between a reform's survival and its slow death.

Honoring the mission versus managing the day-to-day. District and school personnel long for stability and take comfort in standard operating procedures. While a reform is new, a mood of experimentation and change may take hold for a while. Eventually, however, organizations tend to settle back into familiar patterns based on expediency and familiarity, even when these patterns militate against the avowed mission. Political pressures, staff turnover, and everyday logistical issues can erode features of a reform that are inconvenient or that are contrary to accepted culture and norms. The challenge to district and school administrators is to keep the mission of a reform at the forefront, while preserving stability in day-to-day operations. Determining which policies and procedures do and don't serve the reform and meet logistical, legal, and economic needs requires ongoing negotiation between district staff.

CONCLUSION

As we have seen, frequent adaptations are a critical part of the reform process. In Mapleton, for example, district leaders responded to low CSAP scores by increasing instructional oversight and insisting that small school curricula align with state standards (see chapter 5). But as Mapleton was developing its plan, not all of the stakeholders anticipated that such measures might be called for. In chapter 2, we quoted a school board member's description of what he wanted from the reform: "What I was looking for was proven educational concepts that are repeatable and go on year after year, automatic. It doesn't require a driver sitting there driving it year after year after year to make it work. It has to be something that's self-sustaining and shows results."

In fact, there is no such thing as a self-sustaining school model. No reform, once set in place, will produce the same favorable results year after year, automatically. All reform is highly contextual. "Proven" educational concepts may fail to raise achievement, the promises of their adherents notwithstanding. For this reason, districts must be prepared to reexamine their assumptions and practices, to experiment with the models they have adopted, and to encourage innovations by teachers and administrators who succeed the founding generation of reformers.

Charlotte Ciancio and her executive team are certainly aware of this. Whereas five years ago 90 percent of the focus was on creating small schools, now 90 percent of the focus is on improving classroom instruction.

Similarly, one of the referenda that failed would have helped reduce class sizes. To some reformers, this might come as a surprise: proponents of small *schools* have not always been proponents of small *classes*. On the contrary: their argument for the financial feasibility of small schools assumed that student-teacher ratios would be about the same in small schools as they were in large ones. "Personalization," one of the key values of the small school movement, was to be attained not by reducing class sizes, but by creating a school community in which all of the students are known. Evidence from chapter 4 indicates that Mapleton has indeed achieved this kind of personalization. But the new push for smaller classes suggests a recognition that such personalization may be necessary but not sufficient to raise academic achievement. Educating students in a small school where teachers know their students promotes a sense of belonging that can increase retention, but smaller class sizes may be needed to improve academic achievement.

Urban school reform in large and small districts deserves to be a national priority. Half of the urban poor who begin ninth grade fail to graduate. Those who do graduate often find themselves unprepared to succeed in competitive colleges and universities or to meet the demands of the workplace. But there are no quick fixes for a problem as vast and intractable as this. The lure of millions of dollars in grant funding for school reform and the unbridled enthusiasm of reform advocates belie the upheaval and frustration inevitably associated with reform—even when the reform turns out to be meaningful and lasting.

Through the small schools movement, external funders and educational partners have infused public schools with money, ideas, and hope to an unprecedented degree. We have shown in this book that even where hope is warranted, enthusiasm and goodwill alone cannot shield stakeholders from the significant challenges involved in implementing reform. Whole school reform remains a gamble for any district. Instead of glossing over the potential obstacles, advocates should prepare stakeholders at all levels to meet the challenges head on, make smart, well-informed decisions, and thereby preserve the spirit of reform and the promise of public education as well.

Research Methods

Our team understood early on that we would be creating a narrative highlighting the experiences and perceptions of various stakeholders involved in the transformation of Mapleton's high schools. Although the district eventually converted all of its elementary and middle schools into small schools, this book focuses only on high school conversions. We were not charged with completing an evaluation, and it has not been our role or intention to provide an independent assessment of the reform's effectiveness. Most of the evaluative data we have included are summaries of statistics analyzed by district administrators and reports from external evaluators. We did analyze some data collected by the Colorado Department of Education, as well as financial records made available by the district.

In the course of our research, we conducted more than seventy-five interviews and focus groups, seeking the perspectives of more than one hundred district administrators, school directors, teachers, students, parents, and community members, as well as school board members, external partners, and state officials. Larry Cuban interviewed Mapleton's superintendent, Charlotte Ciancio, three times, and we conducted several follow-up interviews with her and her executive team. Documents consulted included two annual reports by external evaluator Dr. Kevin Welner, executive team memos to the school board, and newspaper and magazine articles.

Selection of interview participants was not random. Administrators to be interviewed were identified based on their role in the district or in a particular school. Teachers and students were selected through a "convenience" or "snowball" sampling technique. All of the administrators we approached agreed to participate. Our access to parents was limited; the few parents with whom we spoke were highly supportive of the school district. A small number of teachers declined to be interviewed. While there may be some perspectives on the reform that we did not capture or that we captured only partially, we have strived to represent faithfully all the perspectives we did encounter.

All interviews were completely voluntary and conducted with written or verbal consent. Nearly all were recorded and transcribed. We are aware that even a well-intentioned narrative can trigger political land mines. For this reason, as noted in the introduction, we have concealed the identities of teachers, students, and administrators. Except in the case of the superintendent, all district personnel are identified by pseudonyms. We have also used pseudonyms for students, board members, and state officials.

Data from interviews and other sources were collected from spring 2006 through spring 2009. We were not on the ground during planning or initial implementation, so our interviews are mostly retrospective. As such, they may not be historically accurate in every detail, but they can be understood to be representative of individuals' reflections and impressions.

Seven small high schools were phased in over a three-year period. The first year (2004–05), the district brought two small schools on line. The second year (2005–06), it added four more. In the third year (2006–07), the district opened another school, but also closed and reopened one of the schools it had started in 2004. From 2007 to 2009, some schools added grade levels or consolidated, so that in 2008 there were six schools serving at least grades 9–12. Finally, another small high school (for eighteen- to twenty-one-year olds seeking to complete graduation requirements) was opened in 2009–10. Schools faced their biggest challenges during their first year, and the district's challenges increased during 2005–06 and 2006–07, when more schools were operating than in previous years.

In writing the story of implementation, we were faced with an unusual narrative problem. Because new high schools were created over a three-year period, the "first year" for any given school could be 2004–05, 2005–06, or 2006–07. In this book, we often refer to "the first year" of a high school's operation without specifying what year that might have been. Although the narrative framework is mostly chronological, we skip around at times, referring to issues that might have been raised in one year and addressed in another. We were constantly aware that we were writing a book for both policy makers and practitioners, so in all cases we have tried to present the issues economically without omitting any pertinent details.

While the issues we raise affected the small schools generally, they sometimes manifested themselves differently from one school to another, or to a greater or lesser degree. For the most part, we maintain a district-level perspective, which necessarily obscures school-level variation. A valuable study could be made of any of the district's high schools, yet we believe that the most interesting and policy-relevant issues are common to them all.

At the heart of Mapleton's reform is the passion and concern that makes for any good story. To preserve these qualities and honor the distinctive voices of the participants, we have included extensive quotations. Apart from some light editing to eliminate false starts, "um's," and "like's," the quotations accurately present the words of people reflecting spontaneously on their experiences.

Notes

Introduction

1. Two recent reform-driven books typify the mainstream of this literature: John Simmons, *Breaking Through: Transforming Urban School Districts* (New York: Teachers College Press, 2006); and Bob Wise, *Raising the Grade: How High School Reform Can Save Our Youth and Our Nation* (San Francisco: Jossey-Bass, 2008).

2. In 2002–03, district administrators envisioned four or five small schools. Several shifts in models offered and grade levels served occurred over the next few years, so that at various times there were two, five, six, and seven small schools. In 2008–09, the district operated six small schools. In 2009–10, there were seven.

3. U.S. Department of Education, National Center for Education Statistics, the NCES Common Core of Data Survey, "Local Education Agency Universe Survey, 2005–2006," Table 1.

4. Bill Gates, "First Annual Letter," January 26, 2009, http://www.gatesfoundation. org/annual-letter/Pages/2009-united-states-education.aspx.

Chapter 1

1. Much of this background is drawn from the Introduction in Larry Cuban, *The Blackboard and the Bottom Line: Why Schools Can't Be Businesses* (Cambridge, MA: Harvard University Press, 2004).

2. For a comprehensive summary of advocacy and opposition to NCLB, see "Assessing NCLB: Perspectives and Prescriptions," eds. Sara Schwartz Chrismer, Shannon T. Hodge, and Debby Saintil, special issue, *Harvard Educational Review* 76, no. 4 (2006). For a typical newspaper article summing up many of the criticisms of NCLB but still showing much support for the law, see Amanda Paulson, "A Shortening List of Failing Schools," *Christian Science Monitor*, November 24, 2004, at http://www.csmonitor.com/2004/1123/p01s02-uspo.htm.

3. The value that the reformers place on differentiation helps account for the abundance and diversity of small school models, which vary significantly in their goals, organization, curriculum, and instruction.

4. Michelle Fine and other progressive small high school advocates have argued strongly that the philosophy of small high schools they champion is simply incompatible with top-down, standards-based reforms. See Michelle Fine, "Not in Our Name," *Rethinking Schools* 19, no. 4 (2005), at http://www.rethinkingschools.org/archive/19_04/name194.shtml.

5. Mario Fantini, *Public Schools of Choice* (New York: Simon and Schuster, 1973); Allen Graubard, *Free the Children* (New York: Pantheon, 1973); Daniel Duke, *The Retransformation of the School* (Chicago: Nelson-Hall, 1978); and Mary Anne Raywid, "Alternative Schools as a Model for Public Education," *Theory into Practice* 22, no. 3 (1983): 190–197.

6. Fantini, *Public Schools of Choice*; Duke, *Retransformation of the School*; Raywid, "Alternative Schools."

7. See, for example, Fannie Weinstein, "Alternative Schools Adapt," *New York Times*, June 8, 1986; and Dusty Horwitt, "Farewell to Hippie High," *Washington Post*, June 13, 2004, W28.

8. See, for example, Fine, "Not in Our Name."

9. Bill Gates, "Prepared Remarks," National Governors Association/Achieve Summit, February 26, 2005, at http://www.nga.org/Files/pdf/es05gates.pdf.

10. Linda Shaw, "Foundation's Small Schools Experiment Has Yet to Yield Big Results," *Seattle Times*, November 5, 2006; see Denise Weeks, "Rigor, Relevance, and Relationships: The Three R's of The Bill and Melinda Gates Foundation," *Northwest Education Magazine* 9, no. 2 (2003): 15–16, 46–47.

11. See the Small Schools Workshop Web site, operated by Mike Klonsky, which lays out the research base for small high schools: http://www.smallschoolsworkshop.org/research.html.

12. Valerie Lee and J. B. Smith, "High School Size: Which Works Best and for Whom?" *Educational Evaluation and Policy Analysis* 19, no. 3 (1997): 205–227.

13. Linda Darling-Hammond, Peter Ross, and Michael Milliken, "High School Size, Organization, and Content: What Matters for Student Success?" *Brookings Papers on Education Policy, 2006–2007* (Washington, DC: Brookings Institution, 2007), 163–203. For studies that raise questions about achievement levels (but not the other widely cited outcomes) of small high schools, see American Institutes for Research and SRI, "Executive Summary: Evaluation of The Bill and Melinda Gates Foundation's High School Grants, 2001–2004"; Catherine Gewertz, "Chicago's Small Schools See Gains, but Not on Tests," *Education Week*, August 9, 2006, pp. 5, 18; and New Visions for Public Schools, "Reforming High Schools: Lessons from the New Century High Schools Initiative, 2001–2006." For studies that seemingly accept any gains in test scores as attributable to small high schools without much inspection of students who are attending these schools of choice, see Patricia Wasley et al., *Small Schools, Great Strides*, which looked at Chicago's small elementary and secondary schools created in the 1990s: http://www.newhorizons.org/trans/wasley.htm. Of course, there are also small high schools, such as Denver's Manual High School and Highline's (Washington) Tyee High School, that have died, been put to death, or simply failed to show the promised gains in academic achievement. See Shaw, "Foundation's Small Schools Experiment Has Yet to Yield Big Results," and Catherine Gewertz, "Failed Breakup of H.S. in Denver Offering Lessons," *Education Week*, March 10, 2006, pp. 1, 18.

14. Joseph Kahne, et al., "Small High Schools on a Larger Scale: The Impact of School Conversions in Chicago," *Educational Evaluation and Policy Analysis* 30, no. 3 (2008): 281–315.

15. Bill Gates, "First Annual Letter," January 26, 2009, http://www.gatesfoundation
    .org/annual-letter/Pages/2009-united-states-education.aspx.
16. Bill & Melinda Gates Foundation, "Reflections on the Foundation's Education
    Investments, 2000–2008," at http://www.gatesfoundation.org/learning/Pages/
    reflections-education-investments.aspx.
17. Philissa Cramer, "Klein: Small High Schools Still Succeeding, and More
    Are Coming," *Gotham Schools* at http//gothamschools.org/2009/06/17/
    klein-small-high-schools-still-succeeding-and-more-are-coming/.

Chapter 2

1. Kevin Welner, quoted in William Symonds, "A School Makeover in Mapleton,"
   BusinessWeek, June 16, 2006, at http://www.businessweek.com/investor/content/
   jun2006/pi20060615_730385_page_3.htm.
2. See http://www.essentialschools.org/pub/ces_docs/about/org/execboard/ted_page
   .html and http://www.essentialschools.org/.
3. See http://www.ed.gov/pubs/ToolsforSchools/avid.html.
4. See Larry Cuban, "A Solution That Lost Its Problem: Centralized Policy Making
   and Classroom Gains," in *Who's in Charge Here? The Tangled Web of School
   Governance and Policy*, ed. Noel Epstein (Washington, DC: The Brookings Institution, 2004), 104–130.
5. Strictly speaking, the Coalition of Essential Schools has not developed a school
   model; rather, it advocates a collection of principles that would be used to design
   a school.
6. William Boyd and Jillian Reese, "Great Expectations," *Education Next* 6, no. 2
   (2006): 50–57.
7. See http://www.whatworks.ed.gov/. The standards for evidence driving the
   methodology for the What Works Clearinghouse are described at http://www
   .whatworks.ed.gov/reviewprocess/standards.html. For arguments and examples
   concerning the difficulties of doing experimental educational research, see Joel
   Levin, "Randomized Classroom Trials on Trial," in *Empirical Methods for
   Evaluating Educational Interventions*, eds. Gary D. Phye, Daniel H. Robinson,
   and Joel R. Levin (San Diego: Elsevier Academic Press, 2005).
8. Larry Cuban, *Hugging the Middle: Teaching in an Era of Testing and Accountability* (New York: Teachers College Press, 2009).
9. Robert Horwitz, "Psychological Effects of the Open Classroom," *Review of
   Educational Research* 49, no. 1 (1979): 71–86; Jere Brophy and Thomas Good,
   "Teacher Behavior and Student Achievement," in *Handbook of Research on
   Teaching*, third edition. ed. M. Wittrock (New York: Macmillan, 1986), 328–375
   (quote is on p. 370). More recently, the report of the National Mathematics
   Advisory Panel said, "There is no basis in research for favoring teacher-based
   or student-centered instruction" in learning math (Tamar Lewin, "Report Urges
   Changes in Teaching Math," *New York Times*, March 14, 2008).

Chapter 3

1. Initially, the only new small school that did not have a primarily constructivist approach was York, a K–12 school with an International Baccalaureate curriculum. In 2007, Global Learning Academy, originally one of two Expeditionary Learning schools, adopted more traditional techniques.
2. As the reform evolved, students were grouped into classes for math instruction.
3. Although 2003–04 was the first implementation year, only two new small schools opened, involving only a small number of secondary teachers. Beginning in 2004–05, most secondary teachers were affected by the reform.
4. Because the district does not disaggregate statistics on extracurricular activity in general for elementary and secondary students, estimates of secondary participation must be inferred. Such estimates over-report actual participation, in part because students who participated in more than one sport or extracurricular activity will have been double-counted.
5. Kevin Welner, *Year Two Implementation Evaluation Report* (2007), 48–49.

Chapter 4

1. Self-reports are useful data but, for many reasons, provide only part of the picture of how lessons unfolded. We did not systematically observe classrooms or ask teachers to keep logs. Direct observation of lessons and analysis of teachers' logs would be essential in determining how much and how deeply traditional classroom practices shifted to student-centered ones.
2. See Kevin Welner, *Year One Implementation Evaluation Report, Small Learning Communities, Cohort 4* (2006), submitted to Department of Elementary and Secondary Education, Smaller Learning Program, U.S. Department of Education; also see Kevin Welner and Jessica Allen, *Year Two Implementation Evaluation Report, Small Learning Communities, Cohort 4* (2007), submitted to Department of Elementary and Secondary Education, Smaller Learning Program, U.S. Department of Education.
3. Welner, *Year One Implementation Evaluation Report*, 24.
4. Ibid., 23.
5. Ibid., 30.
6. Patrick McQuillan, "Memo to the District" (2005); cited in ibid., 24.
7. Kevin Welner, *Year Two Implementation Evaluation Report* (2007), submitted to the Mapleton School District, 21.
8. Ibid., 9.
9. Welner, *Year One Implementation Evaluation Report*, 15.
10. Ibid., 15.
11. Welner, *Year Two Implementation Evaluation Report*, 9.

Chapter 5

1. From Charlotte Ciancio, "Overview of 2007 CSAP and ACT Results," memo presented to the Mapleton school board, August 5, 2007.
2. This achievement gap is characteristic of U.S. high schools generally. See, for example, Daria Hall and Shawna Kennedy, *Primary Progress, Secondary Challenge: A State-by-State Look at Student Achievement Patterns* (Washington, DC: Education Trust, 2006), http://www.eric.ed.gov:80/ERICWebPortal/custom/portlets/recordDetails/detailmini.jsp?_nfpb=true&_&ERICExtSearch_SearchValue_()=ED490942&ERICExtSearch_SearchType_0=no&accno=ED490942.
3. See Gary Lichtenstein, "A Call for High School Reform," (Denver, CO: Colorado Children's Campaign, 2003).
4. We analyzed the SST logs documenting every SST visit from October 2006 through April 2009 for four small high schools (MESA, Early College, Welby New Tech, and Skyview Academy). On May 4, 2009, Gary Lichtenstein and Larry Cuban went on SST visits to two of these four schools.
5. Memo from the executive director of learning services to superintendent Ciancio on School Support Team visits, February 5, 2007. Learning walks or walk-throughs are urban district office techniques developed in the past decade to collect evidence that can be communicated to school staff about school climate and the degree to which curriculum standards, teaching, and learning are being pursued in classrooms. See Jane David, "Classroom Walk-throughs," *Educational Leadership* 65, no. 4 (2007): 81–82.

    After Mapleton staff received training from consultants on how to do walk-throughs for SST visits, one top administrator thought that gathering data while on a visit would be far more productive if every SST member had a Palm Pilot. The devices were bought and distributed to teams. Within a few months, the Palm Pilots were no longer used by SST members because, according to the superintendent, the on-site demands of the visit were out of sync with the technology, which proved cumbersome. (Interview with Charlotte Ciancio, May 4, 2009)
6. Kevin Welner, *Year Two Implementation Evaluation Report* (2007), submitted to the Mapleton School District, 15.

Chapter 6

1. See Colorado Department of Labor, "Front Range Foreclosures," *Denver Post*, May 10, 2009, at http://www.denverpost.com/frontrangeforeclosures?appSession=456167602615448. Also see Becca Stewart, "Thornton Reports Third Highest Foreclosure, Unemployment Rate in Colorado," *Examiner*, May 3, 2009, at http://www.examiner.com/x-6583-Thornton-Examiner~y2009m5d3-Thornton-reports-third-highest-foreclosure-unemployment-rates-in-Colorado.
2. See Martin Haberman, *Star Teachers of Children in Poverty* (Indianapolis: Kappa Delta Pi, 1995).
3. Ibid.
4. Interview with SST member, May 4, 2009.

About the Authors

Larry Cuban is professor emeritus of education at Stanford University. His background in the field of education prior to becoming a professor included teaching high school social studies in inner-city schools for fourteen years, directing a teacher-education program that prepared returning Peace Corps volunteers to teach in urban districts, and serving seven years as a district superintendent. He has published extensively on issues related to school reform at all levels, from primary grades through graduate school. His most recent book is *Hugging the Middle: How Teachers Teach in an Era of Testing and Accountability* (Teachers College Press, 2009).

Gary Lichtenstein is owner and principal of Quality Evaluation Designs (QED), a firm specializing in education evaluation and research. He is also Consulting Professor of Engineering at Stanford University, where he specializes in research methods in a national study of engineering education. He worked at the University of Denver from 1993 to 2007, where he directed teacher education, taught courses on research methods, and conducted research and evaluation for the Colorado Community-Based Research Network (CCBRN). From 2002 to 2004, he was director of research and evaluation at the Colorado Small Schools Initiative, an intermediary of the Bill & Melinda Gates Foundation. His intellectual interests include school reform, engineering education, mixed methods research, and community-based research. He can be reached by e-mail at garyl@stanfordalumni.org.

Arthur Evenchik is a former literacy tutor, writing teacher, and program coordinator at the Maya Angelou Public Charter School in Washington,

D.C. He began his teaching career as a writing instructor with the Johns Hopkins Center for Talented Youth, and he has taught writing and literature at the Illinois Mathematics and Science Academy, Goucher College, and Towson University. For seven years, he served as editor at the Institute for Philosophy and Public Policy at the University of Maryland. Currently, he is Assistant to the Dean for Special Projects in the College of Arts and Sciences at Case Western Reserve University, where he oversees a peer-tutoring program in writing and engages in outreach to the Cleveland Metropolitan Schools.

Martin Tombari is a senior research associate at Quality Evaluation Designs and was formerly a senior research analyst at the Colorado Foundation for Families and Children. He received his doctorate in educational psychology from the University of Arizona. He has been a professor at both the University of Texas at Austin and the University of Denver, teaching courses in research methods and statistics. Currently he is directing a three-year study, funded by the Office of Juvenile Justice and Delinquency Prevention, examining the link between peer victimization and truancy in secondary schools. In addition, he is helping evaluate a joint effort by the Adams County District Attorney's Office, the Adams County Public Schools, and Adams County Social Services to reduce school truancy. He has done extensive consulting with schools and mental health agencies to help them carry out both summative and formative evaluations of their programs.

Kristen Pozzoboni is a doctoral candidate in educational psychology at the University of Colorado. Her research interests include adolescent development, youth participation in school reform, and community-based research. Currently, she provides training and professional development in youth development and resiliency theory, policy, and practice. Prior to pursuing her doctorate, she served as an experiential educator for the National Outdoor Leadership School and as a program coordinator for the Division of Educational Leadership at Santa Fe Community College.

Index